International Trade Centre
Training the Trainers

UNCTAD CNUCED   WTO OMC

Training and Consulting

Designing, developing and delivering training and consulting interventions

Geneva 2005

ABSTRACT FOR TRADE INFORMATION SERVICES

<table>
<tr><td>2005</td><td>F-12.10
TRA</td></tr>
</table>

INTERNATIONAL TRADE CENTRE UNCTAD/WTO
Training and Consulting: Designing, developing and delivering training and consulting interventions
Geneva: ITC, 2005. xiii, 158 p.

Handbook on training and consulting skills, aimed at trainers providing business development training and counselling services to SMEs in developing countries – addresses designing, managing and delivering training and consulting services; comprises following modules: 1: The learner and the learning environment. 2: Counselling and consulting. 3: Designing training programmes. 4: Tools for trainers. 5: Delivering training programmes. 6: Managing training programmes.

Subject descriptors: **Training, Business management, Consulting services, Manuals.**

English, French, Spanish (separate editions)

ITC, Palais des Nations, 1211 Geneva 10, Switzerland

The designations employed and the presentation of material in this publication do not imply the expression of any opinion whatsoever on the part of the International Trade Centre UNCTAD/WTO concerning the legal status of any country, territory, city or area or of its authorities, or concerning the delimitation of its frontiers or boundaries.

Digital image on the cover: Lauréna Arribat, ITC

© International Trade Centre UNCTAD/WTO 2005

All rights reserved. No part of this publication may be reproduced, stored in a retrieval system or transmitted in any form or by any means, electronic, electrostatic, magnetic tape, mechanical, photocopying or otherwise, without prior permission in writing from the International Trade Centre.

ITC/P182.E/TSS/EMDS/05-I

ISBN 92-9137-291-9
United Nations Sales No. E.05.III.T.5

Preface

This handbook for trainers and consultants was designed for use in the National Capacity Building programme offered by the Enterprise Management Development Section (EMDS) of the International Trade Centre (ITC).

This programme is designed to address the difficulties encountered when providing business development training and counselling services to SMEs in developing countries. A major cause of these difficulties is the absence of teams of qualified trade or business counsellors. The objective of the programme is to help institutions responsible for supporting SMEs to improve their capacity by developing teams of trainers to train both other trainers and consultants.

EMDS has defined a process for achieving these objectives, which is described in Guidelines for Building National Teams of Trainers and Counsellors. This process defines three sets of skills and knowledge that professional trainers and counsellors should acquire in order to: (1) diagnose management problems; (2) design a portfolio of training and consulting services to address these management problems; and (3) manage the administration, logistics and financing of these services.

The first step in this process, diagnosing management problems, is addressed by training in the Business Management System (BMS) and several analytical tools based on the BMS. The BMS is a model for managers, which enables them to integrate all aspects of business management by matching the strategy and objectives of an enterprise with its marketing and production capabilities.

This handbook addresses the second and third steps of this process, that is, designing, managing and delivering training and consulting services. The six modules in this handbook are divided as follows:

❑ Module 1: The learner and the learning environment

❑ Module 2: Counselling and consulting

❑ Module 3: Designing training programmes

❑ Module 4: Tools for trainers

❑ Module 5: Delivering training programmes

❑ Module 6: Managing training programmes

These modules are intended as a resource for trainers and consultants. Readers are strongly encouraged to view them as a basis for further research and learning in the areas that are most relevant to them, using the abundant literature available on these topics.

Acknowledgements

This handbook was written by Marie Antoinette Orsini, ITC consultant. Viviane Lowe edited the text. Alison Southby carried out an editorial review, and Isabel Droste was responsible for copy preparation and final copyediting.

Contents

Module 3

Designing training programmes

Module 4
Tools for trainers

Module 5
Delivering training programmes 95

Appendices

Thematic bibliography

Tables

Figures

The learner and the learning environment

Introduction

What I hear, I forget,
What I see, I remember,
What I do, I know.

The purpose of this handbook is to assist you as a consultant or trainer in the task of helping people in organizations to gain the knowledge, skills and attitudes that will increase their chances of success. It is not the final word, though; you should also refer to the abundant literature available in order to refine the skills that you need to help and advise businesses and public enterprises. We provide a bibliography to assist you in further research.

This handbook provides the skills, methods and tools you need to be an effective consultant or trainer, particularly in the context of business management. The services you may be providing to your clients basically fall into three categories:

❑ *Consulting*: providing clients with analysis, information, ideas, techniques, tools, know-how and processes which will add value to their performance.

❑ *Counselling*: providing clients with tools and processes that will allow them to find the solution to their problems or the means to achieve their objective.

❑ *Training*: transferring skills, knowledge and tools that can be used in the workplace.

Often the outcome of a consulting intervention can be to advise the client to acquire further skills and expertise through training. On other occasions, you might suggest services which are within your area of expertise or that the client can obtain from other consultants. Whichever the case, at every step of the collaboration you need to show expertise, analytical skills, knowledge of the consulting and training process, a broad understanding of business, and versatility in dealing with groups and individuals.

Like a potter works with clay or a mason with bricks and mortar, the consultant or trainer works with people, alone or in groups. People skills and an understanding of human nature and interpersonal dynamics are the key to success in these fields. You will find that the career you have embarked on is one of constant learning: not only about business management techniques, but also about organizational psychology, human development, and … yourself. You should never consider yourself an accomplished consultant or trainer, but work perpetually towards this goal. Your aim should be to constantly grow and learn.

One thing is sure: whether consulting, counselling or training, you will be working hard to get people to change what they currently think and do, to work differently, and, with luck, to work better and more successfully.

As a trainer, sometimes you will have trainees who are self-motivated and eager to learn. Sometimes they will be less motivated, perhaps even resistant, especially if they are being forced by their company to follow the programme. As a consultant you will often be facing clients who want to improve their processes, but are not willing to change anything in the way they are used to doing things.

The fact is that most people do not easily or willingly give up what they know in order to adopt new ways. Change and learning for adults may imply a gap in their knowledge, a crack in the façade of competence.

Training and counselling adults successfully is quite a bit more difficult than giving good advice or presenting a few good theories. How often is good advice taken anyway? Rather than provide you with 'the' magic formula, therefore, this handbook points you in the right direction by presenting common best practices, methods, techniques and tools that will help you overcome the difficulties frequently encountered in the 'business of change'. Too often we hear that *organizations* should change. But the fact of the matter is that organizations are nothing but the sum of the individuals that compose them. So it is not organizations that change, but *people* within the organization who change. This is why we begin this module with a discussion of the human factor in learning.

In this module, we will cover a number of basic concepts that should be familiar to any trainer, consultant or counsellor:

❑ Specificities of adult learning;

❑ Motivation of adult learners;

❑ Learning styles;

❑ Group dynamics;

❑ Facilitation;

❑ Organizations and learning.

Specificities of adult learning

Part of being effective as a trainer involves understanding how adults learn best. Compared to children and teenagers, adults have special needs and requirements as learners. Although this may seem obvious, adult learning is a relatively new area of study known as andragogy (as opposed to pedagogy). The pedagogue presumes that 'if I said it in a lecture, then they must have learned it'. The professional trainer and developer of human resources recognizes the absurdity of this assumption. The andragogue presumes that 'if the learner has not learned, the teacher has not taught'.

Many trainers enter the adult education field after working as schoolteachers or university professors. They arrive with a baggage of assumptions about how learning is organized, possibly including:

❑ Mandatory attendance;

❑ Public funds pay for education;

❑ Teachers and administrators have *in loco parentis* power;

❑ A wide degree of standardization is imposed;

❑ Curriculum is chosen entirely by officials;

❑ Knowledge is precisely divided into disciplines;

❑ Control of learner behaviour is strongly enforced;

❑ The teacher sets the pace of learning;

❑ Tests are used to measure learning;

❑ Punishment is part of the teaching process.

Many of these conditions will not be acceptable to adults, because adults are motivated and controlled differently in a learning situation. Malcolm Knowles, a pioneer of adult education during the 1950s, identified the following six characteristics of adult learners:

❑ Adults are *autonomous* and *self-directed*. They need to be free to direct themselves. Rather than act as 'teachers' or 'professors', trainers must serve as facilitators, actively involving the adult in the learning process. As facilitators their role is to guide learners to tap into their own knowledge rather than just supplying them with facts. They should ask for suggestions of topics to cover, let the participants work on projects that reflect their interests, and give them responsibility for presentations and group leadership. Finally, trainers should show learners how the training will allow them to reach their goal.

❑ Adults have accumulated a foundation of *life experiences* and *knowledge* that include work-related activities, family responsibilities, and previous education. They need to connect learning to this knowledge or experience base. To help them do so, trainers should draw on participants' experience and knowledge that is relevant to the topic.

❑ Adults are *goal-oriented*. Gone are the days of sitting on school benches studying subjects simply because they contribute to our general knowledge. As adults, we learn with a goal and a purpose in mind. Therefore at the end of the effort, the goals and the gains should be tangible.

❑ Adults are *relevancy-oriented*. They must see a reason for learning something. Learning has to be applicable to their work or other responsibilities to be of value to them.

❑ Adults are *practical*, focusing on the aspects of a lesson most useful to them in their work. They may not be interested in knowledge for its own sake. Trainers need to be clear about how the lesson will be useful to them on the job.

❑ Like all people, adult learners need to be shown *respect*. Trainers must acknowledge the wealth of experience that adult participants bring to the classroom. Adult learners should be treated as equals in experience and knowledge and allowed to voice their opinions freely in class.

Motivating the adult learner

What motivates adult learners? Typical motivations include a requirement for competence, an expected job promotion, job enrichment, a need to maintain old skills or learn new ones, a need to adapt to job changes, or the need to learn in order to comply with company directives. There are at least five factors that are sources of motivation for adults:

❑ *Social relationships:* to make new friends, to meet a need for association, or to make connections and networks.

❑ *External expectations:* to comply with instructions from a superior, to meet the expectations or follow the recommendations of someone with formal authority.

❑ *Personal advancement:* to achieve higher status in a job, secure professional advancement, and stay abreast of competitors.

❑ *Escape or stimulation:* to relieve boredom, provide a break in the routine of home or work, to stimulate creativity, to get new ideas.

❑ *Cognitive interest:* to learn for the sake of learning, seek knowledge for its own sake, and to satisfy an inquiring mind.

Barriers and motivation

Adults who have strong motivations to learn may still experience barriers to learning. Unlike children and teenagers, adults have many responsibilities that they must balance against the demands of learning. Because of these responsibilities, adults have *barriers against participating in learning*. Some of these barriers include lack of time, money, confidence or interest, and scheduling problems.

The best way to motivate adult learners is to simply *enhance* their reasons for enrolling and *decrease* the barriers. Trainers need to find out why their students are present in either their course or the meeting (the motivators); they also need to discover what is keeping them from learning. Similarly, consultants have to understand what is motivating their clients to use their services and discover what is keeping clients from accepting their recommendations and opinions.

Learning tips for effective trainers

There are four critical factors that must be addressed to ensure that adults in the programme will learn effectively: *motivation*, *reinforcement*, *retention* and *transference*. These factors are described below.

Motivation

If the participant does not recognize the need for the information (or has been offended or intimidated), all of the trainer's efforts to assist him or her to learn will be in vain. The trainer must establish a rapport with participants and prepare them for learning; this provides motivation. Trainers can motivate students in several ways:

❑ *Set a feeling or tone for the lesson.* A friendly, open atmosphere shows the participants the trainer will help them learn.

❑ *Set an appropriate level of concern.* The level of tension must be adjusted to meet the level of importance of the course objective. If the material has a high level of importance, a higher level of tension/stress should be established in the class. However, people learn best under low to moderate stress; if the stress is too high, it becomes a barrier to learning.

❑ *Set an appropriate level of difficulty.* The degree of difficulty should be set high enough to challenge participants but not so high that they become frustrated by information overload. The instruction should predict and reward participation, culminating in success.

❑ *Give feedback.* Learners need to hear back from the trainer on the results of their efforts. Feedback must be specific.

❑ *Provide a reward.* Participants must also see a reward for learning. The reward does not necessarily have to be monetary; it can be simply a demonstration of the benefits to be realized from learning the material. Interest is directly related to reward. Adults must see the benefit of learning in order to motivate themselves to learn the subject.

Reinforcement

Reinforcement is what happens when an external stimulus brings about learning. Any method that trainers use to encourage a desired behaviour is reinforcement.

❑ *Positive reinforcement* encourages an attitude, behaviour or performance of an action by providing a reward. The expectation of the award increases the likelihood that the trainee will continue to show the desired attitude, behaviour or performance in the future.

❑ *Negative reinforcement* also encourages an attitude, behaviour or performance of an action by removing something unpleasant that the trainee expects to have to do (for instance repeat the exercise, or stay on after the session for extra practice).

❑ When trainers are trying to change behaviours (replace old practices with new), they apply both positive and negative reinforcement, with a clear preference for the former.

❑ Reinforcement should be used on a frequent and regular basis early on in the process to help the students retain what they have learned. Later, reinforcement should be used only to maintain consistent, positive behaviour.

Retention

In order to benefit from learning, students must retain what they learn in the programme. The trainer's job is not over until he or she has assisted the learner in retaining the information. In order for this to happen, learners must see a meaning or purpose for the information. They must also understand and be able to interpret and apply the information. This understanding includes their ability to assign the correct degree of importance to the material.

The degree of retention is directly affected by the efficacy of learning. Simply stated, if the participants did not learn the material well initially, they will not retain it well either. Practice also increases the likelihood of retention. Trainers should therefore emphasize the importance of practicing new skills or behaviours in order to maintain the desired level of performance.

Transference

Transference of learning is the ability to use the information taught in the course in a new setting. This is the ultimate aim of training. As with reinforcement, there are two types of transference: *positive* and *negative*.

❑ *Positive transference*, like positive reinforcement, occurs when the learner uses the behaviour taught.

❑ *Negative transference*, like negative reinforcement, occurs when the participants do not do what they are told not to do. This results in a positive (desired) outcome.

Transference is most likely to occur when the following conditions are met:

❑ *Association:* participants can associate the new information with something that they already know.

❑ *Similarity:* the information is similar to the material that participants already know; that is, it revisits a logical framework or pattern that is familiar.

❑ *Degree of original learning:* the learner acquires a high proportion of new concepts or skills.

❑ *Critical attribute element:* the information learned contains elements that are extremely beneficial (critical) on the job.

Trainers must remember that learning occurs for each individual as a continuous, life-long process. People learn at different speeds, so it is natural for them to be anxious or nervous when faced with a learning situation. Attention to these four critical elements of learning on the part of the trainer will greatly enhance the likelihood of success.

Learning styles

Not only should you be aware of the characteristics of adult learners in general, you should also keep in mind that individuals have different learning styles. For example, some people retain information that they hear in a lecture, while others must read the information in an article or infer it from experiments in order to retain it. You will address a group of machine operators differently from a group of scientists, because their educational and occupational background will make them receptive to different teaching methods and tools.

The theories of learning styles are based on theories of learning which try to offer possible explanations for behaviour: Why are some people prone to action while others are more incline to reflection? Whether by imparting knowledge, skills or expertise, the idea behind training is to change the behaviours of the participants who attend a course. In order to do so you need to be acquainted with various models and theories of how and why people learn.

There are more than 50 major models of learning styles, all of which have a great deal of congruence and overlap. One of the most widely used and accepted is David Kolb's theory.

Theories of learning styles

Kolb showed that learning styles could be seen on a continuum running from concrete experience to active experimentation:

❏ *Concrete experience:* being involved in a new experience.

❏ *Reflective observation:* watching others or developing observations about own experience.

❏ *Abstract conceptualization:* creating theories to explain observations.

❏ *Active experimentation:* using theories to solve problems or make decisions.

Hartman took Kolb's learning styles and gave examples of how one might teach each of them:

❏ For the *concrete experiencer*: offer laboratories, field work, observations or trigger films.

❏ For the *reflective observer*: use logs, journals or brainstorming.

❏ For the *abstract conceptualizer*: lectures, papers and analogies work well.

❏ For the *active experimenter*: offer simulations, case studies and homework.

Although Kolb thought of these learning styles as a continuum that one moves through over time, usually people come to prefer, and rely on, one style above the others. And it is these main styles that trainers need to be aware of when creating instructional materials.

Basics of group dynamics

Whether consulting or training, you may be facing groups as small as 4 or 5 individuals, or as large as 100 or even 1,000 people.

Dealing with individuals is one thing; dealing with a group is a totally different matter. It is important that you understand the characteristics of adults as learners; it is also essential that you acquire an understanding of the group as a key tool to stimulate the learning process.

Just because a group of individuals have come together under the leadership of a trainer or consultant, does not mean that they are necessarily ready to produce maximum results. The maturity of the group and its readiness to undertake activities, discussions, brainstorming or problem solving depend on certain conditions being met. The trainer must be aware of the dynamics in the classroom, and understand when and how he or she can best use them.

A group is composed of individuals, and, by virtue of the infinite variety of human nature, every group is unique. The group is a pool of knowledge and expertise to capitalize on; it is also the best learning tool you have at your disposal. However, groups obey laws, which seem to be recurrent. It is important to understand some of these behavioural laws of groups so that, as a trainer, you can best use the group to help the individuals within it grow and meet their learning objective.

Understanding group dynamics will help you avoid some classic mistakes, like expecting active participation from the first minute. Similarly, if you wish to involve your participants in group exercises, whether discussion groups or problem-solving groups, it is important that you give time for the group to form and find its mode of operation.

Laws of group behaviour

Charles H. Cooley[1] was the first sociologist to classify groups in two broad categories:

❑ *The primary group:* is a community of individuals united by a communal life, stable and tight relationships (for example, the family, the clan).

❑ *The secondary group:* is a community of individuals gathered around common objectives and linked by formal relationships.

Between 1951 and 1971, Kurt Lewin[2] (who is often referred to as the father of group dynamics) published numerous studies based on a series of sociological, psychological and psycho-sociological experiments on the way in which individuals integrate into groups. According to both Lewin and Cooley, an individual will progressively modify his or her behaviour as he or she becomes part of a secondary group, such as a group brought together for a training programme. This tendency is called conformism. Conformism is motivated by two fundamental human needs: the need for security and the need for approval.

The pressure to conform

All groups tend to put pressure on their members to conform: to unify behaviour, opinions, perception, information, understanding.

This pressure to conform comes from the need for approval, love and security that we feel from the moment we are born. These innate needs are still with us as adults and we will often prefer to sacrifice our own beliefs for the sake of not being rejected by a group.

The need for certainty. Doubt and uncertainty are feelings that cause us pain. Under the pressure of the group, driven by the need for certainty, individuals will often go with the majority rather than express an opinion that differs (and even assume that they must be wrong).

---

1   Charles Horton Cooley, *Social Organization: A study of the larger mind*. New York, Charles Scribner's Sons, 1909.
2   Kurt Lewin emigrated from Germany to the United States in 1923. He was part of the Gestalts school and studied 'the psychological field of the individual'. In 1945 he established the Harvard Center for Group Dynamics. He is considered the father of the experiential learning school Outward Bound.

The need for recognition. People want to be recognized and valued by other group members and by the trainer. A lack of recognition, and the frustration this causes participants, is at the root of 80% of problems in training.

As a trainer, consultant or facilitator, you need to be aware of the pressure the group can exert on the individual and the tensions and the negative feelings that may ensue. Your role is to help the group grow so that it can offer the best possible learning environment. Tensions are part of this growth process; you can't eliminate them, but you can learn to defuse the tensions and put participants at ease.

Tension can be caused by:

❑ Anxiety (expressed by silence, inhibition, or laughter);

❑ Latent conflict or overt conflict between two persons, either because of clash of personalities, or for leadership to dominate the group;

❑ The opposition of the group with its leader;

❑ Repressed frustration, irritation, scapegoating, revolt against rules.

Often groups tend to deny their frustrations and tension until they blow up spectacularly or dissolve into chaos. The trainer's role is not to police the group: he or she should intervene only if the situation really prevents the group from working efficiently. The trainer who takes a strong stance against a member or portion of the group risks making everyone feel that he or she is taking advantage of a position of superiority. As a result the whole group may unite against the trainer. It is much wiser to give the group the responsibility for solving their problems. The trainer can help the group do this by using the technique of questioning, so as to reflect back to the group what he or she sees, and guide them to finding a solution.

As a trainer, you need to follow some simple rules of behaviour:

❑ Put yourself on the same level as the group;

❑ Show patience and tolerance for the process (time is of the essence);

❑ Give the group space, time and decision-making power to solve their problems themselves.

Stages in the life cycle of groups

In addition to the fundamental needs and pressures that guide individuals, groups also grow and change over time. As they grow, they tend to follow a similar pattern. Understanding these patterns will help you make the most of the group in the learning process. There are several models that describe the life of a group – some define four phases, other authors define five phases. In the discussion below we provide several standard names for these phases.

First phase: creation – orientation

During the first hour of existence of your group you will notice that people look, compare, judge, evaluate who they are with, and wonder how they fit in. In this first stage, which is the insecurity stage of the group, the participants try to figure out where they will belong and how they will gain acceptance. The trainer can do a lot to help this process along by emphasizing commonality and throwing bridges between people. Very early on in the introduction, the trainer or facilitator should mention that the present group will become a learning 'team' during the programme.

There are a few little tricks that can help break the ice and put people at ease. We encourage you to use presentations, name games, or other activities that encourage participants to speak to each other. It is important that people introduce themselves with their roles, their functions (their status), but also reveal something of their personality.

Second phase: belonging – progressive opening

It is only when participants understand where they are, with whom and for what purpose, that they can build a sense of belonging. In the first phase, individuals are not linked to each other. In this second phase, they start feeling united at least around a common objective. At this stage, the group can start to be utilized as a learning tool, and sharing of opinions, ideas, and experience can take place openly and freely.

It is up to the trainer to define and impose some basic rules of communication: listening, accepting ideas without criticism, commenting and building upon each other's ideas in a positive manner. This fosters mutual trust.

The trainer will be a role model and will make sure that, at some point during this phase, the group gives itself some basic rules of behaviour that help create a positive learning environment. In the second phase, people are still shy, on their best behaviour and rather individualistic.

The trainer will have to observe the group thoroughly, probe people, reassure, and give positive feedback and encouragement. At this stage, working in small groups is often quite effective.

Third phase: development of participation – freeing the tension – storm

After a while, participants will feel more at ease with each other, and will start speaking more freely. They are reassured and feel they belong to a unit that accepts them and makes them grow. At this point, the natural tendencies of individuals will take over, and participants will start arguing with each other and freely expressing disagreement. Once we know we are accepted, we feel freer to be ourselves. Such behaviour will become more evident if you involve the group in problem solving or in a task activity. Under the pressure of time or the pressure to perform, the tension will start to come out. At this point, the group will also try to find out the best way to organize itself.

The trainer will act like a coach, a role model and a facilitator to help the group identify some of the best practices or some of the principles they should apply to be most efficient.

A group becomes efficient when it goes beyond the third phase.

Fourth phase: maturity – the structuring of the group reaching group cohesion – norming

This phase is the blessed phase for the trainer. The group has found a modus vivendi that allows it to get the best out of the sum of its parts. The various roles of its members are known and accepted, strengths have been identified, and people know how to get the best out of each other and themselves.

At this point, the group is ready to take charge of itself and be autonomous. It knows how to assess its evolution, assess its strengths and weaknesses, regulate internal tensions, and handle pressure from outside.

At this stage, the role of the trainer is that of an outside observer who can still provide insights and inputs.

Fifth phase: the death of the group

The course is over: everyone takes back his or her identity independent of the group. The death of a group is often a very sad event. It is important to make it meaningful so that people keep good memories of the training. Trainers should think about how to make the end of training meaningful, symbolic and engaging. It is always good to think about the 'after training' phase and create anchor points to which people make commitments.

The classic description of group life can be represented graphically as an ascending stairway as in figure 1.

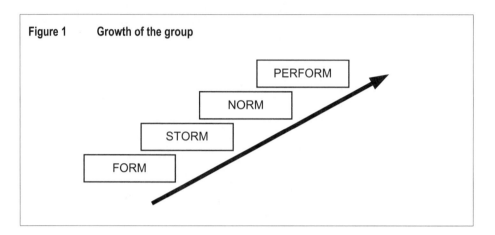

Figure 1   Growth of the group

An understanding of group dynamics helps to clarify the role of the trainer or facilitator and define the behaviour and attitude that is most appropriate for the learning growth of the group.

❑ Trainers should always be clear about what type of intervention they are conducting – teaching or facilitating? The ability to alternate between the two techniques is key to success.

❑ The goal for the trainer or facilitator is to bring the group to a level of maturity where learning will take place – too many groups stay stuck in the first phase, observing each other warily without interacting, or at the third phase, where confrontations and arguments are more important than real learning. In order to bring the group to a level of maturity where it can perform, the trainer will sometimes have to withdraw from confrontation with one or several participants and leave his or her pride aside.

❑ The facilitator or trainer should always show the group where it stands on the learning curve, and how much it is progressing towards the learning objectives of the programme. Feedback should be honest, and if it is critical, should be accompanied by guidance.

❑ The trainer or facilitator should always verify that the methods of work that he or she has chosen for a given objective are suitable. This self-analysis requires flexibility, the mastery of a variety of methods and tools, as well as the ability to improve.

Working with the group

When leading meetings or activities you need to be aware of three things: purpose, process and product. This simple model can be applied to everything: a meeting, a task, an activity or a training programme.

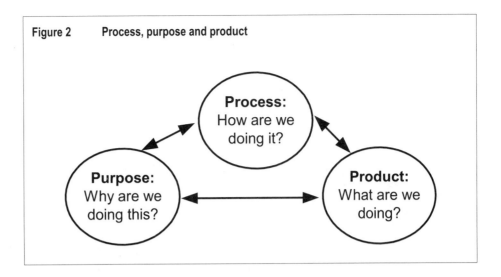

Figure 2   Process, purpose and product

❑ *Purpose:* Why are we doing this? Why are we having this meeting, why are we doing this analysis?

❑ *Product:* What are we doing? Are we discussing, are we deciding, are we solving a problem?

❑ *Process:* How are we doing it?

The 'how' questions describe the process. Processes are the 'soft' parts of a task: the way we communicate, the way we decide, the way we share information and select our action, the way we solve conflicts, manage crises, the way we lead or accept leadership. In most tasks, the process is like the bottom of the iceberg that no one sees but that can cause severe damage.

This term process is also used in engineering and manufacturing. It describes the various stages and phases a product or service has to go through. Human beings also have processes in learning, as we have seen. Though more subtle and difficult to identify for a novice eye than the processes of manufacturing tables and chairs, they are no less essential.

These concepts apply to training and consulting, as much as they do to management. You will realize that many managers, though expert at what they do, frequently forget to pay attention to how they lead, how they talk to their employees, how they take decisions.

The success of the consultant or trainer depends on his or her ability to apply the right process with the client or group he or she is dealing with, and to understand when and why a process is not at its best and what should be improved. When training you need to be able to read the group so that you know what is required for each situation.

Basics of facilitation

Facilitation may be a new term to you. Sometimes facilitation is considered a technique, sometimes a skill, and at other times a profession. Let us assume it is all of this in one. Facilitation is not teaching, it is not training, nor is it consulting, but it is a 'tool' you apply in teaching, training and consulting interventions. It is a way of providing leadership without taking over the reins. It is, in fact, the best tool you can use with adults in a situation where they have to learn to take decisions. It will be your key instrument in your job. A facilitator's job is to get others to assume responsibility and to take the lead.

The facilitator's role

As a consultant or trainer you will spend some of your time acting as a facilitator. So what exactly do facilitators do? A facilitator can perform any of the following tasks:

❑ Help a group define its overall goal, as well as specific objectives;

❑ Help a group assess its needs and create plans to meet them;

❑ Provide processes that help the group use their time efficiently to make high-quality decisions;

❑ Guide group discussion and keep them on track;

❑ Take notes that accurately reflect the ideas expressed;

❑ Help the group understand its own processes in order to work more effectively;

❑ Make sure that assumptions are made explicit;

❑ Use consensus to help a group make decisions that take all members' opinions into account;

❑ Support members in managing their interpersonal dynamics;

❑ Provide feedback to the group members so that they can assess their progress and make adjustments;

❑ Help the group communicate effectively;

❑ Create an environment where members enjoy a positive and growth-enhancing experience.

As you can see, facilitation has everything to do with enhancing the group's and each individual's capacity to discuss, decide and get the most out of each other.

To be a good facilitator you need to dose your input carefully, so that the majority of interaction takes place between participants.

❑ Frequent interventions from the facilitator decrease the level of participation of the group;

❑ The more the facilitator expresses personal opinions, the more participants will talk to him or her and the less they will exchange and interact;

❑ For the affective and intellectual life of the group, and for objectives to be met, it is best if participants have a high level of interaction;

❑ The facilitator's remarks (when opportune and well formulated) can favour and improve these interactions.

The role of the facilitator as described above does not follow the 'expert model', where the consultant has all the answers and provides all the solutions. However, to be able to apply your knowledge and your solution, you will need to get from your clients and participants as much information as possible. To do this, you also need to engage them and earn their trust. In order to take the best decision for the firm you are working with, you need to create a consensus or make sure all suggestions have been explored. For this you will use facilitation skills.

Questioning techniques

One of the key tools of facilitation, which will be essential to consulting, is questioning. The art of questioning is one that matures with time, experience, practice and knowledge. The better you will become at questioning the better you will be at your job.

Simple do's and don'ts apply to questioning. The objective is not to appear smarter than the person you are questioning but to collect information of quality. As long as your purpose is to acquire the information you need, questioning has to be very straightforward.

Do	*Don't*
• *Be prepared – decide beforehand what questions you will ask.*	• *Improvise your questions on the spot.*
• *Ask clear, concise questions covering a single issue.*	• *Ask ambiguous questions that cover multiple issues.*
• *Ask challenging questions which stimulate thinking.*	• *Ask questions that do not provide an opportunity for thinking.*
• *Ask reasonable questions based on what the person is likely to know.*	• *Ask tricky questions designed to fool the person.*
• *Ask honest and relevant questions.*	• *Use complex or jargon-filled language.*

There are four types of questions you can ask:

Closed questions can be answered by yes or no or by providing information. You ask closed questions when you are looking for specific information. If you feel the question will be considered too direct, preface it by explaining why you need this information.

How much do you sell per year? Who is in charge of sales? Is company X a supplier of yours?

Open questions are answered by in an explanation, a description, a history or an analysis. In order to clarify certain details provided in the answer to an open question you can follow on with some closed questions.

Can you describe your distribution network? Why do you think there is a problem with quality?

Probing questions are open, but prepare the ground for the answer. The interlocutor knows what you think and might tend to go along with your point and provide you more information. Or he or she may contradict you and provide you with different opinions and facts.

I understand from what you told me that you have difficulty with the quality of this product. What is your view on this?

Hypothetical questions require the interviewee to think about a hypothetical situation. You are trying to acquire information in an indirect way. You think your interlocutor might give you information that he or she would withhold if you asked a more direct question.

Let us assume you would be entering this new market. What would the effect be on your production cycle?

At the end of the interview, you may close the discussion with some leading questions. These are questions that are formulated to suggest an answer in agreement; they are searching for confirmation. You usually state your position and opinion on the issue you have discussed and ask what the interviewee thinks.

As a consultant, you will also have to answer many questions. Here again, a few simple rules apply:

❑ Be honest if you don't have the answer. Too often, people fake an answer or beat around the bush. Be simple, direct and if you need more time to think about it, say so. *Let me think about your question and get back to you later...*

❑ Use the P-R-E-P model:

P – state your Point: what is your position?

R – state the Reasons for your point

E – give Examples that will support your reason

P – restate your Point

In module 5 we provide you with more techniques for facilitating and for engaging groups in discussion.

Organizations and learning

As we have seen, the work of a trainer or consultant is closely linked with the learning process. How people learn is in turn dependent on the dynamics of the group. One such group is the organization. It is, therefore, essential to understand how the organization might promote or hinder learning.

Chris Argyris[3] argues that if organizations allowed and encouraged individuals to develop to their full potential it would be beneficial to both parties. 'Many companies that aspire to succeed in the tougher business environment of the 1990s must first resolve a basic dilemma: success in the marketplace increasingly depends on learning, yet most people don't know how to learn.'

Similarly, Peter Senge[4] wrote that 'for organizations to survive in the future, their capacity to learn has to be equal or greater than the rate of change'.

In fact, learning and organizations do not go hand in hand easily. You may deliver management and leadership skills programmes but they will not necessarily result in the improvement of the skills of managers and leaders in the organization. This is because there are many factors, such as company structure, culture and hierarchy, that make organizations resist change and learning.

The structure

The barriers to learning in an organization can be linked to its organizational and hierarchical structure. If the organization can be represented as a pyramid, hierarchy sets up barriers between the 'floors' of the pyramid as in figure 3. Senior management, middle management and workers are all concerned with maintaining their respective positions in the pyramid and resist suggestions or ideas coming from the other levels.

Companies are also composed of many different departments. We can imagine them as silos. The lack of communication between the silos creates organizational barriers to information sharing and effective learning.

---

3   Chris Argyris, *On Organizational Learning*. Blackwell, Cambridge, 1993.
4   Peter Senge, *The Fifth Discipline: The art and practice of the learning organization*. Doubleday, New York, 1990.

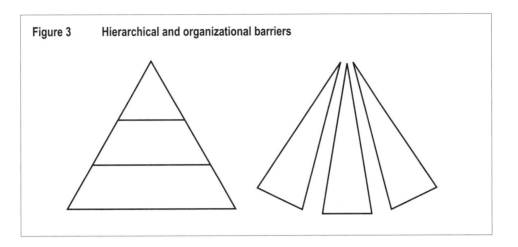

Figure 3   **Hierarchical and organizational barriers**

Operating culture

The culture of the enterprise may also act as a barrier to learning. Learning requires flexibility and a willingness to risk something. Managers everywhere are not always ready to accept new ideas, particularly if they have not been tested. An operating culture where fear and blame are in place will definitely not favour new thinking. The worry for managers will be 'What if it fails? I will take the blame and may lose my job'. Similarly, a very hierarchical culture, where people are afraid to take responsibility and always defer to the boss, will not encourage innovation and change.

Power and control

Often people are afraid of change because they feel insecure about their position and power. The fear of losing power is a main cause for resisting change. For an insecure manager, letting a subordinate attend a course where he or she will learn new skills that the manager may not have will be perceived as a threat.

People in an organization often feel disempowered. They feel that they have limited responsibility over what is taking place and as a result they defer to their hierarchy for any major decision or responsibility. In SMEs or family-owned businesses employees do not always feel it is appropriate or useful for them to speak up. This will be another interesting dimension to watch for. Working as a consultant for these types of business can be more satisfactory as it may lead quickly to effective results, but it may also be more frustrating, as the resistance to new ideas can be stronger and less diffused than in big corporations.

As consultants and trainers we repeatedly face such challenges. A consulting assignment relies on the ability of the system to integrate new ways of thinking and new ideas. Organizational barriers make it difficult, and are, therefore, something we will have to watch out for.

Module 2

Consulting and counselling

Introduction

What is a consultant? One could say that doctors, lawyers, architects, psychologists and advertisers all provide a consulting service. That is, they give advice, make recommendations, and offer tools and services that fill a need or help solve a specific problem for their client. This is exactly what business and management consultants do. They make a living out of offering their knowledge and expertise to enhance the capabilities of their client's company. Their work should lead to quantifiable or perceivable improvements for the client.

A consultant should be able to operate in organizational structures as diverse as a bank, a hospital, a non-profit association, a manufacturing company, a government institution, a school or even a cooperative.

In this module we will define the role of the consultant; describe in detail the processes of a consulting project; and provide you with some of the tools that you will use in the course of a consulting project.

Reasons for retaining consultants

Businesses and organizations use consultants for many different reasons. A few of them are discussed here. See appendix I for a more complete list of the areas of specialization of consultants.

To define and achieve objectives

The company or organization may have set objectives, such as achieving excellence in serving customers, increasing competitive advantage, implementing total quality management, or achieving higher productivity, higher performance and profitability. The consultant's role may be either to help the company define these objectives and decide how they will be achieved, or only the latter. The consultancy has to add value to the organization, in the form of tangible and measurable progress towards the objective.

If the consultant is to be successful in helping the client reach these goals, a crucial condition is that the goals be well defined. When this is not the case, the consultant's role will be to first help define the goals and make sure they are the most appropriate ones for the company – at this point in time and in future – as well as to ensure that they are properly communicated and endorsed by key members of the organization.

To solve management and business problems

The consultant's role is to assist with his or her experience in diagnosing and solving management or business problems. These can be a whole range of issues met in the course of managing a business: high staff turnover, personal conflicts, low quality, loss of market share, cash flow problems, resistance to change, poor customer satisfaction and so on.

Some of these issues are causes of a problem, while other are the symptoms of a problem whose cause needs to be determined. The skill of the consultant will be to define exactly what the problem is, and to avoid taking what the client requested at face value.

To innovate and seize new opportunities

Sometimes consultants are called on to help develop new products or new markets, to improve quality, or to identify new business opportunities.

To enhance learning

Clients may approach consultants to acquire new knowledge, technical skills or operating methods, to develop process improvement and acquire methods to assess their organization. They may also wish to develop management, problem solving, public speaking or communication skills and so on. This type of consulting does not resolve any particular problem but helps develop the company and the satisfaction of the employees.

To implement changes

There are a whole range of consulting firms known as change agents who help companies to understand change and create a culture where change is accepted as a way of life. The organization wants to understand and make the required modifications, which will help its survival in the dynamic environment in which it is operating, and calls on a consultant to facilitate this process.

Types of consulting companies and services

In any consulting job, there are two parties who interact with each other: the client and the consultant. The consulting process should help the client resolve a problem or improve a situation. To achieve this, the client must choose the consultant that is best qualified to meet the company's needs. The key question for the client, then, is: *What kind of consultant should I choose?*

There are essentially five consulting styles, as defined by Larry Greiner and Danielle Nees.[5] Each will be appropriate to a different type of management or operational issue. Their characteristics are summarized in table 1.

'The intellectual adventurers'

These firms aim at providing companies with 'scientific' solutions to complex problems. They collect large amounts of quantitative and qualitative data and analyse them in a scientific manner. They act on the basis of a solid know-how, built over years of experience. They do not provide key-in-hand solutions, but rather a sum of analysis and information, which may not always be directly applicable to the company.

Arthur D. Little, the Rand Corporation and the Batelle Institute are some firms that fall into this category.

'The strategic navigators'

These firms provide advice on the strategic orientation of the company. They take a holistic view of the company, which encompasses technology, economic environment and sales. They gather data on the company, and use economic models to analyse organizational phenomena, assess the relationship between the company and its environment and suggest new strategies, markets and opportunities.

Boston Consulting Group (BCG), Bain, and Braxton are some firms that fall into this category.

'The management doctors'

These consultants take a systemic view of the company. They look at the organization and all its components – structure, strategy, processes, procedures,

---

5   Larry Greiner and Danielle Nees, 'Conseil en management : tous les mêmes?' *Revue française de gestion* No. 75, November-December 1989.

mission, values, management style, know-how – and provide a sound analysis and diagnosis. They identify the problems of an organization, and through a fairly open process try to elaborate solutions. Once a solution has been chosen, they help with the implementation.

MacKinsey & Company falls into this category.

'The system architects'

These consultants are the technicians of management. They intervene to rationalize the management system and the decision-making process. Often they are specialized in a specific area of management, such as compensation, evaluation, knowledge management, supply chain or Total Quality Management. System architects do not take a holistic view of the company, but intervene only on the basis of diagnosis in the specific area of their competence.

Accenture, Booz Allen Hamilton, Ernst and Young, and Hey consultants fall into this category.

'The friendly co-pilots'

Often a small consulting firm or even consultants working alone, the 'co-pilots' work individually with their clients, and tend to develop close long-term relationships with upper management. They are usually not area experts, but have a generalist management background. They provide advice and assistance on a variety of management issues.

Table 1	Consulting styles				
	Intellectual adventurer	**Strategic navigator**	**Management doctor**	**System architect**	**Friendly co-pilot**
Background	Scientist	Economist	Manager and administrator	Area specialist	Management
Role	Research	Plan	Diagnose	Conceptualize	Advise
Method	Statistical analysis	Modelling based on key variables	Holistic analysis of company and processes	Propose and implement solutions	Personal assistant to top management
Focus	Creative solutions	Objective setting for the future	Organization and strategic objectives of the company	Management procedures	Wants and needs of top management
Client expectation	Solutions based on well-researched information	Identifying profitable niches and markets	Improving organizational efficiency overall	Improving efficiency in a chosen area	Improving decisions of management

Companies may rely on consultants to:

❑ Provide market information;

❑ Provide specialist skills;

❑ Establish business contacts and connections;

❑ Offer expert opinions;

❑ Diagnose problems;

❑ Develop action plans;

❑ Elaborate systems, methods and procedures;

❑ Plan and manage change;

❑ Train management and personnel;

❏ Counsel and coach managers;

❏ Provide intensive professional help on a temporary basis;

❏ Justify management decisions.

Client–consultant relationship

As we have seen, companies and organizations may turn to consultants for a wide variety of problems. Their interaction will then generally follow one of three possible models: the expert; the doctor/patient; or the process consulting model.

The expert model

The consultant is considered as an expert bringing in a specialist knowledge. He or she is expected to provide solutions that the company could not find on its own with its internal resources. Using an expert requires the client to:

❏ Identify the problem very accurately;

❏ Select the right consultant with the right area of expertise;

❏ Communicate to the consultant all the information needed to understand the problem;

❏ Accept the conclusions of the consultant, and deal with the consequences of the change to be implemented.

The doctor/patient model

The consultant is called on to diagnose the problem and prescribe a cure. The consultant becomes responsible for planning the whole project. The danger in this relationship, is that the client may be tempted to transfer to the consultant many of the responsibilities for the change, expecting him or her to provide a painless 'miracle pill', when in fact the client will have to take responsibility for 'curing' himself or herself.

The process consulting model

In this model, developed by Edgar Schein in the 1970s, the objective is not to provide turnkey solutions but to help the client identify the problem and find the resources to solve it. The client becomes responsible for the change he or she will implement. This model is based on the principle that clients have, within their organization, the knowledge and know-how to solve their problems. It is then a matter of applying the right process to make all the elements of the solution emerge and then plan the actions. The difference between the expert model and the process-consulting model is similar to that between consulting and facilitating (see module 1 for a discussion of facilitation).

What style to choose

The style of consulting you adopt will also depend on the nature of the problem, as we have seen, but also on the type of client you have. There are major differences between an SME and a big corporation in the nature of the relationship the consultant can establish with the company. In SMEs, the fact that the owner has such a major role makes him or her the main actor in the consulting process, which is positive if he or she is deeply committed to pushing through changes. However, he or she may also be the main source of the problem, which makes it all the more difficult to negotiate a solution. In contrast, in big corporations it is often difficult to meet and get involved with the key decision-makers. Not only is there a dispersion of responsibilities, but also it may be more difficult to assess the impact of an action on the organization.

Essential skills for consultants

There is no foolproof recipe or standard career path to becoming a consultant. However the common trait of most good consultants is a passion for business and a flair for interpersonal relations. Too many consultants are good technicians but lack the fundamental interpersonal skills to be able to communicate, listen and convince. In this section we will discuss what skills you need to develop and cultivate to succeed in the consulting game.

The first skill is to be able to *listen*. Consultants listen not only to what is being said, but also to what is not being said. They have an active listening ability, and constantly question and rephrase to refine their understanding. Often consultants think their role is to fix problems quickly, so they jump too quickly to proposing a solution. They feel that they are not giving the client his or her money's worth unless they bring him or her answers, models or tools. This is wrong. You will find that often questioning and active listening provides most of the answers.

The second skill is *adaptability*. You will need to adapt to working with all sorts of people, in many industries and in widely varying situations. The consultant should be able to establish contact and enter into working relationship with a broad range of individuals, from workers to managers, from entrepreneurs to civil servants. You will adapt by adjusting your language and terminology, the speed of your reasoning, the subject of conversation and your knowledge of a particular industry. Adaptation requires curiosity, learning, research and investigation. As a consultant, you are a constant learner.

The third skill is to be able to play the fine balance between *being a diplomat* and *being direct*. During a consulting assignment, you often need to involve several parties with diverging interests; to make this happen you need to negotiate consensus and buy-in without threatening anyone. By the same token, you have to be convincing and articulate when stating your position; you must be able to tell the truth without offending anyone and you must involve everyone.

The fourth skill is *intuition and sensitivity*. Although a consulting assignment should be based on facts and data objectively analysed, you should also sometimes rely on your intuition. Intuition may tell you that the manager has misdiagnosed the cause of a problem, and that you need to speak to some other people in the company to get a clearer picture. Sensitivity will help you manage difficult interpersonal situations without creating bad feelings or making enemies.

You also need to cultivate qualities of *patience and perseverance*. Clients sometimes take time to make decisions. They may also wonder how to get approval from the right people. Be patient, do not lose faith, and give them time to adapt and to adjust. As a rule of thumb, the gestation period to acquire a new client is nine months.

Those skills will be enhanced over time, if you cultivate them through constant reflection and self-evaluation. Many people consider these 'soft' skills unimportant. On the contrary, they are a key ingredient. Lest we forget, organizations are not machines and procedures, they are people operating machines and applying procedures. So, consultancy is at heart a business of people.

On top of those interpersonal skills there are other qualities a consultant should have. The most important is *integrity*. Integrity means behaving according to a high standard of honesty and respecting a code of ethics.

As a consultant, you are in a business relationship with a client who entrusts you with sensitive information about his or her company. A basic ethical rule is that you treat information with discretion and confidentiality. Whenever you can and if you have doubt, clarify whether you are dealing with sensitive information or if it is in the public domain.

Ethics also require you to deal fairly with the financial side of the relationship. Be sure you keep the financial terms clear on both sides.

It is unethical to misrepresent yourself: you have to be honest about what you can and cannot do. Do not offer your services if the situation is outside your area of competence. You may associate yourself with a knowledgeable person in the field, or recommend someone else to do the job, but do not pretend to be more than you are. Your client will be thankful to you in the long run.

You should always be honest about what you think. You may find out during your diagnosis that the issue you were presented with is the effect and not the cause of the problem. Say what you believe and have the courage to voice your opinions even if it means losing the contract. Do not accept a job if you think the service you have been asked to provide is not essential or is even counterproductive. It will be a waste of money for the client, and you risk being seen as a parasite who is taking advantage of the situation. This is particularly true when providing training services: many consulting firms milk so-called 'cash-cow programmes' that are non-essential for the company's employees but are steady money-spinners for the consultants.

As a consultant, you will have to manage many frustrations. Sometimes you will be brought into a meeting where the agenda is not clear. Sometimes your contact will give you information and will describe the mission to you in one way, while during a meeting with his or her boss you will be given a very different picture. On other occasions, you may fail to convince your client of your position. Consulting is fraught with frustrations, and it requires confidence to continue nonetheless.

Although it is important to be confident in your opinions and abilities, it is just as important that you be able to question your assumptions. Self-reflection is part of the job; just as you expect your client to learn and grow, you will have to do the same. We encourage you to develop your self-knowledge either through introspection or by regularly attending courses. If you are a self-employed consultant, you should make an effort to attend retraining seminars, and evaluate the quality of your work with colleagues or with clients. In consulting firms, regular 'train the trainers' programmes should be delivered to develop the competency of all employees.

See appendix II for a summary of the essential skills of the consultant.

The consulting process

The classic description of the consulting process divides it into five phases:

❑ Entry and discovery;

❑ Diagnosis and analysis of the problem or situation;

❑ Action design;

❑ Project and implementation;

❑ Termination and evaluation.

Each phase is interconnected and the quality of one will impact the quality of the others. The phases are summarized in table 2. In table 3, the steps and success factors for each phase are discussed further.

As you can see from table 3, each step of the consulting process is made up of sub-steps and depends critical factors for success. We will look at some of these steps in further detail. At each step of the process, you need to assess whether you have done the right things, whether the step is complete, whether the right people have been involved and whether you have all the information, resources and tools to move to the next step. In the next sections we will discuss each phase in greater detail.

Table 2	Phases of the consulting process
Phase	**Description**
Entry and discovery	• Initial contact with the client. • Diagnosis of the problem from the client's perspective. • Planning of the project for proposal.
Pre-diagnosis	• Planning of the project for proposal. • Drafting of proposal and pricing. • Contract.
Diagnosis and analysis	• Fact finding. • Analysis of facts and synthesis. • Detailed discussion with client and confronting of the analysis (from the client's perspective and consultant's perspective).
Action planning	• Developing solutions. • Evaluating alternatives. • Proposal to the client. • Planning and implementation.
Project and implementation	• Assisting with implementation. • Assisting with communication and information to employees. • Adjusting proposal if required. • Training staff if required. • Transferring knowledge and information.
Termination and evaluation	• Evaluation. • Final report. • Setting commitment. • Plans for follow-up. • Closing contract and payment.

Table 3	Steps and success factors in the consulting process	
Phase	**Steps**	**Critical success factors**
Entry: Understanding the request	• First contact. • Discuss the client's perception of the problem or the need for help. • Explain how the consultant might help. • Clarify the expected contribution of each party.	• Listen critically to the client's description of the situation. What is hiding behind the words? Challenge the client's analysis. • Make sure you are not the instrument of a single person in the company. • Ensure that the right decision-makers are involved in the process. • Do not assume you are the right consultant for the project.
Pre-diagnosis	• Perform preliminary analysis and diagnosis of the client's problem. • Prepare a project plan based on first hand diagnosis. • Draft a proposal and contract.	• Ask for access to more than one point of view; take time to deepen your understanding even if you want to contract.
Diagnosis: Gaining insight	• Identify the nature of the problem: technical, information, structure, processes, external, skills related, psychological, etc. • Use several forms of investigation: interviews, observation, group facilitation, surveys, etc. • Share your analysis with more than one person; accept being challenged. • Write up your analysis.	• Learn to omit certain facts but to look for others. • Make sure to differentiate between the cause and the effect. • Take more time if necessary. • Don't look for bears if there aren't any! • Do not raise expectations which may lead to disappointment and upheaval. • Never point a finger at anyone in particular. • If the project is outside of your area of competence, say so.
Planning: Finding the solution	• Find alternative solutions and evaluate each of them. • Draft a plan of action. • Present your proposal to the client.	• Be creative and use your imagination. • Be rigorous and systematic in your approach. • *'When you are good with a hammer you see everything as a nail'*: do not just apply your expertise as the key solution; there may be others. • Evaluate the impact of your plan at each step and understand whose support you need in the company – then enrol and convince them. • Eliminate proposals that lead to unnecessary changes.

Implementation: Testing the solution	• Break your plan up step by step and understand expected output at each step.
	• Monitor the quality of services at each step.
	• Verify understanding of what is going on – from a client's perspective.
	• Get feedback from the client at each step.
		• Intense presence with the client and constant dialogue will be key.
		• Divergence from planned results (versus actual results) can be due to:
		  – Incorrect assumptions;
		  – Incorrect fact gathering and subsequent analysis;
		  – Incorrect diagnosis;
		  – Organizational resistance;
		  – Unforeseen obstacles;
		  – Planning errors;
		  – Incorrect implementation;
		  – Over-estimation of results.

	Table 3 (cont'd)	
Phase	**Steps**	**Critical success factors**
Termination	• Evaluation of the consultant's approach. • Evaluation of the consultant's performance. • Assessment of the changes made and their actual results. • Planning for follow-up and assignment of responsibilities. • Final report. • Payment of services.	• Spend time evaluating and debriefing the process, the people and the manner in which the consulting was done. Evaluate with your client but also with your team. • Write a report only if necessary but do plan for an evaluation session. • Make sure invoices are sent promptly and in agreement with the client. • Keep information on file about what you have done.

Entry phase – first contact

This is the crucial phase where you will make your first impression on the client. Too often, this first meeting is handled poorly. Consultants arrive in the firm without a clear idea of what the agenda of the meeting is, what the client expects, and how long the meeting will last. It is essential to clarify these issues beforehand because it helps harmonize the consultant's and client's expectations. So, as a rule of thumb, prior to meeting a client for the first time, or meeting for the first time on a new project, make sure you find out:

❑ What is the purpose of the meeting?

❑ What does the client expect?

❑ How should you prepare, and what materials should you bring?

❑ How much time is allocated?

The first contact prior to the meeting, often by phone, is an opportunity to introduce yourself, be discovered and make a sales pitch. However, you should be aware that some clients who are not used to the consulting process might expect you to come with ready-made solutions. Avoid this potential unrealistic expectation by stating what the purpose of the meeting is.

In the first meeting, both parties get to know each other better. There is no rule as to who should speak first. If you are the one making the sales pitch, you should start. If it is the client who requested your services, he or she should speak first. Let the client speak as long as he or she wishes. You may decide to follow on with some questions to deepen your understanding of what he or she said, or to introduce yourself, highlighting why you are the right person to talk to.

Introducing yourself is something you should rehearse time and time again, in front of colleagues, spouse and friends. It is always fascinating to see how people close to us will ask the 'silliest' question that we have the hardest time answering. The clients will do so as well. You need to master how you present your services and have a clear picture of what you can contribute to the client.

In front of the client, however, you will adapt your presentation so that it fits the situation he or she will have introduced. You will need to give examples of similar work you have done elsewhere, how you did it, and how it is relevant for the present situation.

Clients frequently need to be educated about what a consultant does. You may need to explain the consulting process, and detail what you will need from them in order to do your job well and what the next steps will be if they retain your services. You should not hesitate during this first meeting to ask your potential clients for their impressions of you and the services you provide.

Clients will seldom give you the go-ahead right away, but they may occasionally do so. In either case, the next step will be for you to go back to your offices and write an offer, detailing how you will proceed to further diagnosis, or if the problem is simple, what consulting solution or process you will offer.

It is important to gather some basic information about the client during this phase. If you have a feeling that the client might hire you, tell him or her already what kind of information you will need to gather in order to refine your diagnosis and prepare a proposal.

The proposal will need to be written a very short time after the first meeting. It should show your professionalism, and reflect your insightful analysis of the situation and your knowledge of the industry. The proposal should include financial terms, a time frame and a fairly detailed plan of how you intend to proceed either to understand the problem or to solve it. All principles applicable to written documentation will be relevant here, namely: good presentation, readable format, and professional appearance. At first, it will take you a while to prepare a proposal, but it will become easier as you gain experience.

Keep track of all the proposals you send; you will find that there is a format that you can reuse often.

Table 4	Tips for the first meeting
Find out some basic information	• The purpose of the meeting. • The time allocated. • The location. • Who will be present, their titles and functions. • Get some background on what the company does, what the project is.
Come prepared	• Bring documentation and business cards. • If the client is expecting a sales pitch, bring materials to make a formal presentation. • Dress professionally. • Make sure your materials are orderly. • If you come with colleagues, decide beforehand who is the key spokesperson. You do not want to contradict each other. When in doubt refer to the spokesperson, or ask if the others agree. • Be on time.
Handle the meeting well	• Ask questions that show your facilitation skills and your natural curiosity. • Don't show off, by using abstract or very academic language for instance. • If your client uses unfamiliar terminology do not hesitate to ask for clarification. • Bring humour and warmth to the meeting. • Bring closure to the meeting by saying what you will do next and clarify who will establish the next contact. It is always best if you are in charge of this: You may just say, 'If you do not mind, I will call you on such and such day, at such and such time; are you available then?'

Problem pre-diagnosis and diagnosis

As we suggested earlier, the client's own diagnosis of the problem may be incorrect or the problem may be poorly defined. You may have to investigate it further before you can make a proposal. This investigation is called a pre-diagnosis.

The time you will spend on preparing a preliminary diagnosis is significant, so this part of your services will have to be paid. You need to make an initial proposal explaining how you will conduct the pre-diagnosis, and make a financial offer. The client will assess your proposal and tell you whether you may continue your research or not.

At the end of your preliminary diagnosis, you have all the elements needed to prepare the final consulting offer. This again may include further research and investigation, which might be more costly and time-consuming. Some problems require comprehensive diagnosis, survey, process mapping and market research.

Common mistakes in problem identification

Both consultants and clients often make some costly mistakes in their diagnosis of problems. Just like a doctor, a consultant observes 'symptoms' and tries to determine the 'illness' or cause. Just like a doctor, he or she can get it wrong.

Confusing cause and effect or symptoms with problems

This is one of the greatest pitfalls for both managers and consultants. To return to the doctor analogy, let us consider a patient whose symptom is headache. The doctor who treats the headache with painkillers, when in fact the patient is suffering from a brain tumour, is mistaking the symptom for the problem. In a company, the symptom could be interpersonal conflicts. The manager might assume the cause lies in conflicting personalities, when in fact the problem is poor role definition (cause), resulting in conflict (effect). If the manager 'treats' the problem by sacking or transferring the troublemakers it will have very little effect on the problem because the root cause remains.

Preconceived ideas about the problem

Often the client or the consultant will view a problem from his or her own angle and may be operating more on intuition or assumptions than on facts. Consultants need to approach a problem with a 'blank slate', and be aware of any biases that they might be bringing to their analysis.

Narrow specialist viewpoint

We like to see the world from our point of view, and it is often an overly narrow one. Engineers see a technical solution for every problem, while lawyers prescribe a legal fix, and quality consultants see quality issues everywhere. Sometimes, technical solutions are the easiest ones to undertake: all you need is to buy better machines and tools, or new computers. However, a purely technical solution overlooks the human side of problems – remember, it is people who operate the machines. This is why consultants need to be as open-minded and holistic in their approach as possible.

Narrow organizational viewpoint

People within an organization also tend to see problems from their position within the structure. Some companies operate with strong silos: departments do not communicate with each other and as a result problems are not tackled in a systemic, company-wide fashion, but department by department. Sometimes, the lack of collaboration or communication between silos is the cause of the problem. If the consultant does not gather perspectives from every department, the analysis may be biased and incomplete.

Incomplete diagnosis

An incomplete diagnosis will result from narrow or overly rapid research, from bias, or from incomplete information.

Where to get the information

Before you can proceed with the pre-diagnosis analysis you need to collect information and data on the company. You may find useful information in:

❑ Written material, documents, annual reports, advertising materials;

❑ Minutes of meetings, plans, decisions, correspondence;

❑ Interviews;

❑ Group discussions;

❑ Observation of plant facilities and offices;

❑ Attendance at meetings and decision-making sessions;

❑ Contacts with clients, distributors and providers;

❑ Examination of products and packaging, service or after sales;

❑ Client complaints;

❑ Questionnaires and surveys.

There are no set rules on how to gather information, but there are a few techniques (more of these will be presented in module 4). It is important to gain a historical perspective on the company, its past and present achievements. Sometimes being able to pinpoint when a company experienced a crucial event, may get you closer to the source of the problem. You also need to know facts and figures and the plan and strategy on which the company is operating.

The first step of your diagnosis is a good general understanding of the client. Only after this should you talk to people to gain their perspective on how they view the problem. However, some consultants like to do both background research and interviewing simultaneously. In certain situations, this may be feasible, for instance if you are conducting a team building, management and leadership training programme. For productivity and process improvement, you need to have a good basis of information first before talking to anyone.

When conducting interviews and meetings, you need to come prepared with a template for transcribing the data. For group sessions, you need to have group processes in place.

The techniques provided by Edgar Shein in process consulting are very useful for interviewing. As we saw earlier, process consulting is based on the assumption that clients have within themselves the knowledge and resources to understand and solve their own problems. It is a matter of providing the right setting and format to create meaningful and honest discussion, so that the expertise and knowledge within the staff will emerge. With this approach the consultant acts mainly as a facilitator.

At every step of your diagnosis, you need to compile your data. Do not leave everything to the end when you will have forgotten much of the detail. Keep good files of the relevant documentation. In some cases, you may want to bring some documents with you to interviews or group meetings so that you can quote facts, statements or financial figures precisely.

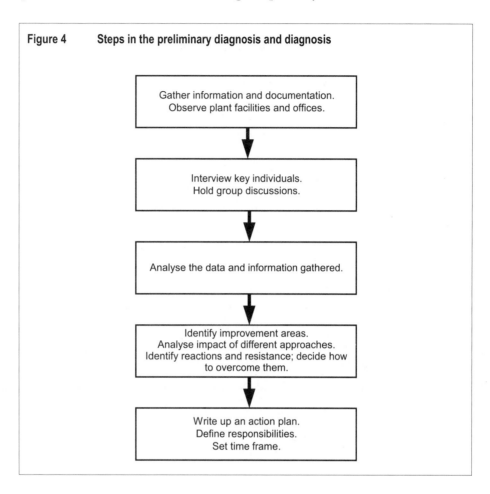

Figure 4   Steps in the preliminary diagnosis and diagnosis

Gather information and documentation.
Observe plant facilities and offices.

↓

Interview key individuals.
Hold group discussions.

↓

Analyse the data and information gathered.

↓

Identify improvement areas.
Analyse impact of different approaches.
Identify reactions and resistance; decide how to overcome them.

↓

Write up an action plan.
Define responsibilities.
Set time frame.

Writing a proposal

Once you have gone through the pre-diagnosis, you are ready to write up the proposal upon which the consultancy will be based. The proposal is, in essence, a plan describing the consultant's strategy for resolving the issues or problems. This will require resources and manpower from the consultant but also from the client.

Your proposal should include the following sections:

❑ A description of the problem;

❑ The objectives to achieve;

❑ The detailed work programme to be undertaken – including need for further diagnosis and actions;

❑ The description of each task in the programme;

❑ The allocation of responsibilities for each step;

❑ The process by which the client will be informed;

❑ The time schedule;

❑ The cost and contractual terms.

The proposal must be written in a clear and professional manner, highlighting matters of importance. The aim is to seal the deal but also to set clear expectations.

Format for proposal writing

Title page

❑ Title of the project;

❑ Name of your contact;

❑ Client's company name and address, and their logo if available;

❑ Consultant's name, company and address;

❑ Name of the training or consulting company;

❑ Date.

Understanding of the situation

Summarize the request for consultation as the client presented it to you. Make sure you use similar language, repeat the stated concerns, the examples given and the purpose of the request.

Analysis of the situation

At this point in your document, you will confront the client request with the preliminary diagnosis you have made. You will state whether you concur with his or her analysis and what your conclusions are. You can voice any doubts you have about the accuracy of the client's analysis and suggest further investigation if you think it is needed. Your analysis of the situation has to be convincing and needs to focus on what could be the benefits of a consulting project as well as its potential outcome.

The proposal

The proposal itself should lay out the steps of the consulting process and detail the expected results. The expected results are the objectives of the project. As you may know, objectives have to be SMART – Specific, Measurable, Achievable and Realistic within a given Time frame. Quantify objectives whenever possible – this makes the proposal clearer.

If your offer indicates that you need to conduct further diagnosis, explain why. If your diagnosis is already complete, you will probably need to communicate your analysis to a number of individuals in the company, and ensure that they buy into it and give you support during the consulting process.

Describe the various tasks your consulting project will require, how you will carry them out, how many workdays it will take, where and with whom consultants will work, and so on.

A consulting project requires work from the client as well: attendance at meetings, research, time spent with the consultant, analysis of processes, etc. You must be very precise about what you will require from the client.

Do not forget to mention who will be the main consultant for the project and who will assist him or her. Provide a short biography of the consultants.

Critical success factors

In this section you describe the responsibilities of the client and that steps that must be taken to ensure the success of the project. Sometimes the critical success factor is simply the dedication shown by top management or middle management to the project, and the way they communicate these changes to employees, suppliers and distributors. You need to state your expectations clearly.

Deadlines and timeline

Provide an overall deadline for the project and a timeline for each step. Indicate what the outcome of each step will be, and the output you will deliver, if any. Sometimes the output may be measurable and quantifiable. Do not produce too many reports or studies throughout the process, but do find a way to keep the client informed of your progress. Make sure that your main contact in the company always knows what you are doing so that he or she is not affected by the rumours that invariably run wild when there is a consultant in the company.

Logistics

Logistical issues include dates, presence of consultants in the company, what they will be doing when present (reading documents, working with employees, analysing data, observing processes, etc.). Make as accurate a calendar as possible. Make sure you specify what resources you expect the company to provide, such as office space, a computer, a telephone or administrative support. Employees can become very resentful if they feel you are unfairly taking advantage of their time. So be sure to clear these details with management ahead of time.

Financial terms

This is where you will provide the financial terms for your services. They should be as detailed as possible. We recommend that you itemize the services in such a way that the client can gain a good idea what the final price is going to be. Transparency always pays off.

There are different pricing methods:

❑ Price per hour;

❑ Price per half day;

❑ Price per consulting day;

❑ Flat fee (all inclusive itemized price).

Preparation days may be billed at a different rate. Use of specific tools, machines, tests, computer programs, instruments is usually billed to the client and should be itemized. If you are the owner of proprietary processes, or of computer programs, you may charge a price for the tool, plus a usage fee.

Travel and living expenses are also charged to the client and should be estimated in the terms. They are, however, paid separately upon submission of receipts. It is important to put a cap on those expenses when they constitute an important part of the budget.

Some consulting firms working on cost reduction programmes have found an interesting way to be paid. They ask for a percentage of the savings they generated for the company. Similarly, consultants who offer solutions to increase market share may ask for a percentage of the sales volumes increase. This, or other forms of 'pay for value' remuneration should be considered only if you are very experienced and confident in the impact of your work.

Don't forget to clearly state the currency and the terms of payment (time, whether cheque or wire transfer, etc.).

There are several possibilities for timing payment. Sometimes consultants are paid in several instalments, with a portion being paid up front, a portion half way through and the final balance on completion. Sometimes the entire fee is paid after the end of the service. The advantage of requiring a partial payment up front is that it gives the client an incentive to maintain its commitment, while providing the consultant with some revenue during the duration of the consultancy.

Specify whether you need a purchase order or a contract. If you want a contract you need to agree on who will write the contract.

Since it can sometimes take a long time for the client to produce a contract, you may request a 'letter of intent' or a 'letter of agreement'. This letter specifies that the client is engaging your services for a particular project and commits to covering your fees until the contract is issued.

Consulting tools

The main purpose of consulting tools is to help you gather and categorize information, then analyse it. They do not provide the solutions, but should be seen as a means to engage people in thinking and to structure the thought process. This means that instead of just taking notes at random on a little notebook, like Sherlock Holmes, you will organize them in a systematic way, using tables, charts and graphs. They can also be very useful for convincing a client or framing a discussion.

There are a vast number of tools that can be used in consulting. You may already have learned to use ITC's NeedSME tool, which helps you organize data according to the key business tasks. You will probably want to learn how to use some other analytical tools as well. We will limit the discussion to a brief presentation of some of the better-known tools: fishbone diagrams, force fields, prioritization charts, simple cause analysis charts and SWOT analysis. Additionally we have reviewed some of the classic survey and audit tools.

Cause analysis chart

This is a grid for classifying data according to the five functions of the business:

❑ Production;

❑ Sales;

❑ Finance;

❑ Human;

❑ Legal.

All decisions in the company must take these five functions into consideration. You will analyse the situation of the client according to these five criteria, or according to any other criteria you consider relevant. For instance you could add technical and scientific criteria in the case of a pharmaceutical company, or financial market information if your client is a bank.

In the first chart (table 5) you list the criteria of analysis and against them list all the facts you know for each area. The second and third columns will be for the results of your analysis.

Table 5	Cause analysis chart		
Criteria of analysis and classification	**Fact**	**Appreciation**	**Proposal**
Production			
Sales			
Finance			
Human			
Legal			

First, however, we will turn to the second information grid in table 6, with which we will organize the analysis of our data. This grid is more complex and will require you to break you data up further – or complete it if you find you are missing a crucial bit of information. What is the company strategy in each area? What are the priorities? Doing this exercise will also force you to question your assumptions.

Table 6	Information grid					
Criteria	**Analysis of facts**	**Prioritization**	**Strategy**	**Tactics**	**Means of action**	**Planning**
Production						
Sales						
Finance						
Human						
Legal						

Once this is done, return to the cause analysis chart and enter your analysis and proposed solutions.

Cause and effect chart

This chart helps you distinguish more clearly between cause and effect (we warned you earlier about mistaking effects for causes). When you are analysing a problem, divide a flip chart sheet into two columns: title the right column 'effects' and the left column 'causes'. If you are working with a group, use the group brainstorming technique you will learn in module 4, and whenever someone offers a point, ask them whether it is a cause or an effect, then write it in the appropriate column.

Fishbone diagram

Use a fishbone diagram to systematically organize all of the factors contributing to the problem being analysed. The cause categories on fishbone charts can vary; usually they include people, equipment, materials, policies, procedures, environment, costs, and so on.

Start by placing the observed effect, or problem, in the head of the fishbone. Determine the major cause categories, and add them as 'rib bones' to the 'backbone'. Then ask members to brainstorm all the possible causes branching off each bone.

Once all of the causes have been identified, ask the group to brainstorm solutions for each of them, or use a voting method to sort the causes according to their priority for being solved. In figure 5 the sample problem is too many defective products. Each of the branches could also have sub-branches of contributing causes. This same model can be used to analyse a process by detailing all the factors that influence it.

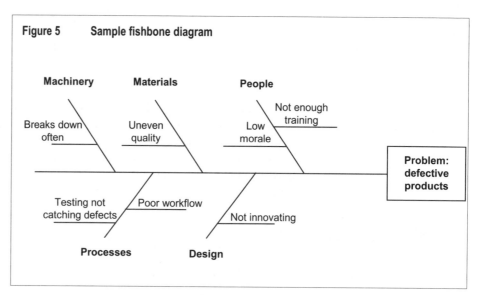

Figure 5   Sample fishbone diagram

SWOT analysis

SWOT analysis is a very old consulting tool; it is also an excellent facilitation tool that you can use in group discussions. SWOT stands for:

Strengths;

Weaknesses;

Opportunities; and

Threats.

Strengths: What are the assets (material, financial, technical, human, creative, environmental) that give the company an advantage?

Weaknesses: What is keeping the company from succeeding? What is lacking or defective in its way of operating, technology, knowledge, etc.?

Opportunities: Where are the opportunities for the company? What niche, new market do we see? Does it have a unique product, or the potential to create one? Every objective, goal or strategy presents opportunities. Those opportunities can be internal and external. Listing them allows us to take a long-term view. It also fosters a positive outlook on the future.

Threats: What are the dangers facing us? What stresses do we have to expect? If our objective is to increase market share, can production cope with the increase in volume? Like opportunities, threats can be internal and external. Looking at the threats allows us to anticipate future difficulties.

When you combine all these elements of analysis you have a reasonably full picture of the situation, which should allow you to capitalize on strengths and identify ways you can transform weaknesses into strengths.

The next step is to look for causes and think about possible solutions, that is, ways to maximize strengths and opportunities or minimize weaknesses and threats. These solutions will be concrete actions (to consolidate strengths or compensate weaknesses) and strategic plans (to position the company so as to benefit from opportunities and fight off threats). Table 7 suggests a matrix format to organize and present the completed SWOT analysis.

Table 7	SWOT analysis grid	
Identify	**Analyse**	**Plan**
Strengths (list them)	Causes	Actions: What can we do to maintain strengths?
Weaknesses (list them)	Causes	Actions: What can we do to eliminate weaknesses?
Opportunities (list them)	Conditions	Strategy: How can we seize opportunities?
Threats (list them)	Conditions	Strategy: How can we anticipate / avoid threats?

There are many processes you can use to conduct a SWOT analysis. You can do it individually, or have several people do it on their own and compare notes. You can use it to structure a group discussion. If you decide to use a SWOT analysis as a process for group discussion, start with a brainstorming session. Then divide the group into four sub-groups. Each sub-group will begin by defining, in precise terms, the objective or the strategy they are working on. After they have spent a few minutes discussing and have come to an agreement, they will each work on the one of the four themes.

You can also present your diagnosis to the client using a SWOT format.

Four organizational assessment tools

Organizational assessment tools include surveys, questionnaires and interviews. You will find many ready-made questionnaires available, but they are not difficult to construct yourself. If you choose to do so, start by identifying the areas you need to survey by gathering a wide range of opinions. Formulate questions carefully, making sure that only one item or issue is associated with each question. You need to ensure that the anonymity of the respondents will be respected. Look at modules 3 and 6 for a lengthier discussion of questionnaire protocol, numbered evaluations and examples of several types of questionnaires.

Processing and then using the data is the main challenge of surveys and audits. Sometimes it is easier to run the questionnaire on a sample, or a small number of people, rather than the entire organization so that you do not have so much data to deal with. This will be your choice. You may also find that your survey asks questions to which you already know the answers, but if this is what is required to convince your client that there is a problem in a specific area, it is worth going ahead with it.

Table 8 outlines the characteristics of four classic organization assessment tools: the climate and attitude survey, the operational audit, the culture audit and the organizational scan.

The planning of surveys and audits is a key factor of their success. Frequently surveys are launched without defining an operating assumption or expectation of what the survey should achieve.

Table 8	Organizational assessment tools			
	Climate and attitude survey	**Operational audit**	**Culture audit**	**Organizational scan**
Purpose	To determine the feelings and opinions that employees have at a given time about an initiative or set of issues.	To determine actual processes, procedures, methods and activities, in order to compare them with those that are documented or imposed.	To determine the values, belief systems and behavioural practices in place: how work gets done, how people behave, etc.	To determine what the issues are, identify the strengths, weaknesses, values and practices, both vertically and across departments.
Scope	Can be limited to a specific issue, or cover a broad spectrum of issues (e.g. what does it feel like to work in this company?)	A broad survey to identify the company's processes, procedures and activities. It may be targeted at the entire company or at a given operation or department.	A broad survey to identify all behavioural factors influencing how and why the company operates as it does. It can be targeted at a specific department or at the whole structure	A very broad survey to identify how the organization operates, what processes and procedures are used, as well as issues surrounding individuals or groups. The main focus is on alignment of all elements within the system.
Method	Questionnaires with either numerical answers (scoring) or multiple-choice answers. Just a few open-ended questions to broaden the data.	Focus groups, interviews, observations, questionnaires.	Facilitated focus groups, interviews, questionnaires.	Facilitated focus groups, interviews, questionnaires, surveys. All of these can be modified if unexpected data emerge.
Target population	Entire population or representative sample.	Key operators in charge of critical processes, procedures or methods. Users of outputs of the processes.	Key representatives of senior management, heads of departments.	Target population of Operational audit and Culture audit.
Use	Helps identify opinions and feelings and determine what problems may require further investigation.	Determine compliance with rules and regulations and whether processes are adequate to achieve the strategy. Determine operational priorities.	Determine cultural strengths, characteristics and strategic fit. Determine the need for cultural change projects.	Determine alignment of the organization as it is operating today.
Product	An academic style report of quantifiable segments and opinions about specific issues.	A descriptive report on the processes, procedures and activities actually operating in reality versus on paper.	A descriptive report on how people interact and communicate and what values they hold.	A descriptive report on processes, structures, company culture and values.

Force field analysis

The force field is a facilitation tool that helps visualize both the factors that contribute to achieving an objective and those that hinder it. Again, like the fishbone or SWOT, it does not provide solutions, but serves as a framework for thought or discussion.

For the chosen goal you will list forces, both internal and external, which contribute to reaching it above the line. Below the line, list the forces that prevent the goal from being reached. At first list the broad categories; in a second stage go into the details of each.

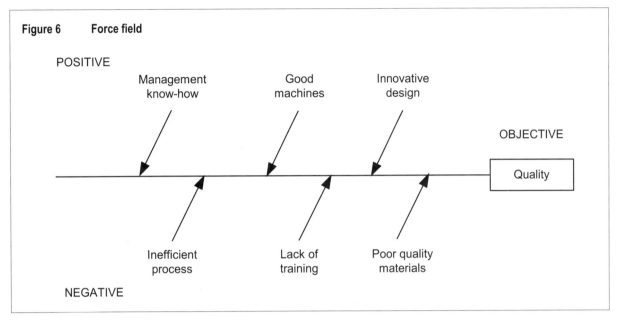

Figure 6   Force field

Once you have listed all the forces, the next step will be to understand the causes of the resistances, or negative forces. How do they manifest themselves? What can we do to redress the situation?

You may refine your force field model by distinguishing between internal and external forces, coding one in blue and the other in green, for instance, or making them the subject of a separate force field chart where the distinction is between internal and external.

Prioritization chart

The prioritization chart is a very simple visual tool that helps classify actions and activities according to two criteria.

For example, let us imagine you are reviewing the tasks of a department. You need to identify which tasks contribute to the department's objectives and which do not, and how much time is spent on each activity. The prioritization method follows in four steps:

❑ List all the tasks performed;

❑ Estimate the time spent on each task;

❑ Rate the task according to its importance for achieving the objective;

❑ Place the tasks into one of the areas of the quadrant in figure 7 according to their level of importance and time required.

You now have a good picture of what the team is doing and how much time and effort is being allocated. How many of the tasks in the lower left quadrant (low priority, less time-consuming) can be totally eliminated? What can be done to reduce time spend on tasks listed in the lower right quadrant, tasks which take a lot of time but which sit low in the priority list? How can we focus on the high priority items while making them more efficient?

Figure 7   Prioritization chart: priority vs time

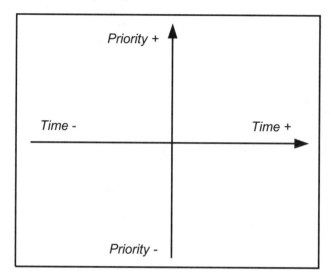

You can use these prioritization charts with any criteria you wish. For instance, the same format could be used in a strategy meeting to classify actions according to the effort they will require versus the impact they will have. Post all ideas for actions on a flip chart and discuss where they fit on the grid in figure 8. All ideas or potential actions would fall into four categories. If you follow the logic, in categories 1 and 2 are actions that should or could be implemented immediately and would yield quick results. In category 3 are actions that would require a detailed action planning but could reward the extra effort, while actions in category 4 should be discarded.

Figure 8   Prioritization chart: effort vs impact

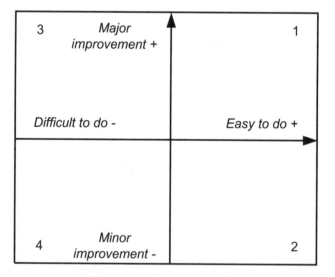

Very quickly you will see which actions require little effort but will have a high impact – these should be taken right away. The actions that will require a lot of effort but will be rewarded by a high impact may need to be analysed further using the prioritization methods described below. The major difficulty in using this grid is to clarify exactly what is meant by the criteria 'easy to do' or 'difficult to do', and what constitutes an improvement.

More complex prioritization charts

You can use prioritization charts to analyse more complex solutions by using more than the two criteria allowed by the methods discussed above.

The first step is to determine the important criteria for your objectives, goals or decisions. Each of those criteria needs to be given a numerical value.

Let us assume you want to choose the most appropriate trainer for delivering very important programmes. You want a trainer who knows the material well, has a good contact with you, the client, and will not cost you too much. To distinguish between the four bids you have received, you rate the candidates according to these three criteria.

Knowledge of the material	0 = no knowledge
	1 = little knowledge
	2 = very knowledgeable
	3 = extremely knowledgeable

Good contact with the client	0 = unknown to the client
	1 = little contact with the client
	2 = good contact with the client
	3 = excellent contact with the client

Fees	0 = very high
	1 = high
	2 = moderate
	3 = low

To rate the candidates you enter their scores into a grid and total the points. According to this method, your best choice is John, whose knowledge and good contact with the client offset his low score on fees (he is more expensive than candidates Fatima and Amelia). You will have noticed that for fees the scale is reversed: the higher the fees the lower the points scored.

Table 9	Prioritization with several criteria			
	Knowledge	Client contact	Fees	Total
Paolo	3	0	0	3
John	2	3	1	6
Amelia	1	2	2	5
Fatima	0	1	3	4

You can apply this method with a larger number of criteria, to rank actions for instance. The criteria could be cost, time, knowledge, skills, resources, etc.

Action planning

It is never easy to move from diagnosis to preparing an action plan and implementing it. The whole process will be based on the quality of the data you have collected, your analytical skills and the willingness of the client to buy in to your suggestion.

Your choice of actions will be focused on developing one or more solutions to the problem diagnosed. You will then evaluate alternatives and choose from them. You will present the proposal to the client, and depending on what he or she accepts, you will plan for the implementation of the solution.

The choice of solutions should follow a clear logic and answer these important questions:

❏ What should the new arrangement achieve? (What level of performance? What quality? What new product or services? What new markets?)

❏ How will the new situation differ from the present?

❏ Are the effects likely to last?

❏ What difficulties are likely to arise? (For instance employee resistance, stress, over-production, shortage of materials, customer resistance, distributor resistance, etc.)

❏ Who will be affected?

❏ When is the best time to change?

❏ What are the financial implications for the company?

Any action you propose will operate within certain parameters: cost is an important one; the capacity of the client to implement those changes with existing resources is another. You also need to understand whether there will be any serious side effects on the rest of the organization. Most importantly, the client should have ownership of the solution, so that he or she does not resist changes.

The reality is that action plans are not easy to follow. Many broad-range consulting projects end up suffering delays, which may have financial implications and a serious impact on the implementation of change. In module 6 we introduce the Gantt chart, a project management tool, which is invaluable for planning complex projects requiring numerous resources and parameters.

Concluding a contract

Although this might seem the least important phase of a consulting assignment, it carries weight for your future work and your reputation. Both client and consultant should part with a feeling of accomplishment. Both also should draw some conclusions from the experience and take the time to analyse how the work was done: what were the results, and what can be learned from it for the future?

Sometimes your consulting proposal will have planned for an evaluation. This may take many forms. The easiest is a final debriefing meeting with all the stakeholders of the project. Other projects may require more complex evaluations, which should only be undertaken if they add some value.

These are some of the questions you might discuss in an evaluation meeting:

❏ What do you need to learn from a consulting project – what is good to have versus what is nice to have?

❏ What kind of recommendation do you need to receive from the client?

❏ What follow-up work should the client do after the project is over to sustain the effort or to keep on improving?

❑ Would you be interested in writing a case study on the project – so that you can use it in your 'portfolio'?

❑ Do you need to give further feedback to your client on things you have seen, observed or heard?

As soon as the project ends, you should invoice the client. The fees will be paid on receipt of the invoice. Make sure this phase is done professionally and swiftly. There is nothing worse for the client than receiving an invoice 12 months late with justification of long-forgotten expenses – you take the risk that your expenses will be rejected by the accountant. You should be able to close the books of a project within 30 days of its termination.

Module 3

Designing training programmes

Planning a training programme

This module will introduce you to the skills and tools you will use to plan and carry out training programmes for clients. The planning stage follows many of the guidelines laid out in module 2 for preparing a consulting plan. In order to plan a programme in detail, it is necessary to first define the objectives clearly. The first step in programme design is therefore to gather information from the client so as to gain a clear picture of the goals of training. Only then can you begin to think of ways to reach them, and choose the methods and tools that will help you do so.

The training system

Figure 9 shows how the elements of a training programme mentioned above relate to each other.

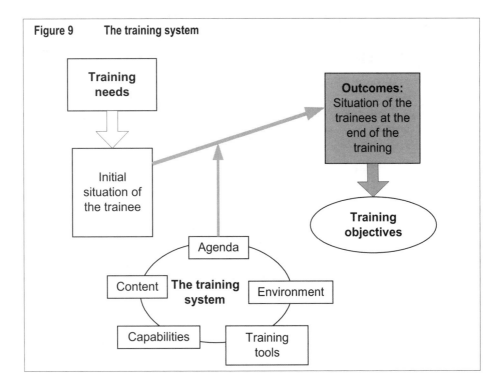

Figure 9   The training system

Training needs need to be clarified first, so this is the starting point. All programmes should be designed either for a need that the trainer or the training company is responding to, anticipating, or even fulfilling based on a market survey, or to respond a specific request from a client.

The training objectives are the expected outcomes of the programme: the knowledge, know-how and attitudes that participants will gain at the end of the programme. They will need to be specified accurately and in measurable and tangible terms.

The outcomes describe what success looks like at the end of the training, when the new skills have been applied.

The training system is made up of all the tools, training materials, plans and environmental factors that contribute to the success of the training (defined as achieving the stated objectives). We have defined five factors:

❑ *The agenda* is the activity plan, the step-by-step sequence and timeline that the course will follow to attain its objectives. It should be defined session by session, following logical steps in terms of content and in terms of pedagogy.

❑ *The content* is the sum of materials, theory, models, information, or new ways of thinking delivered in the course. It is what the trainer expects participants to learn.

❑ *The training tools* are the techniques for communicating content: various exercises and group activities that the trainer will use to communicate the content and to involve participants in its delivery.

❑ *The capabilities* of the trainees to assimilate the content of the course are an important factor as well. Therefore, the skills, abilities and attitudes of programme participants should be evaluated beforehand. These are influenced by factors such as culture, education, present position, ability to articulate knowledge, receptivity to new ways of thinking, and willingness to be challenged and to work in groups.

❑ *The environment* is every outside condition that influences learning: whether the participants are colleagues or not; whether the programme is taking place in a company or outside; the classroom set-up; etc.

These elements fit together in a sequence, as shown in figure 9. Planning a programme involves the following tasks (although you may order them differently):

❑ Clarify the programme needs;

❑ Understand the purpose of the programme based on the needs you are trying to fulfil;

❑ Develop programme objectives that you know can be met;

❑ Determine what capabilities are required for the programme;

❑ Decide on learning content and material;

❑ Develop the schedule step by step and session by session;

❑ Design your programme by selecting or designing your tools;

❑ Decide whether you want to use evaluation or assessment tools to verify participants' learning.

Each of these steps will be discussed further in this module.

Collecting information

The first step in training design is to analyse the needs and wants of a client. This involves not only understanding the needs of the client, but also becoming familiar with the client's industry, the job descriptions within the company, the profile of the employees you will be training and the environment within which they operate.

There are several methods for collecting the information you need to make an accurate needs assessment. We will review eight different techniques, which can be used in conjunction with NeedSME, the needs assessment tool provided by ITC.

The client's request for training must be analysed from a very broad perspective. The course designer must search for the root of the problem, and must decide how to respond to the client's request in such a way that the training programme will have a real added value. For this to happen the designer will have to start by evaluating the job environment and performing what is called an organizational analysis.

The client organization may have many reasons for requesting a training programme. These are a few examples among many possible situations:

❑ Some workers are failing to perform some aspects of their job in a satisfactory manner. The purpose of the training would be to help these workers improve their performance.

❑ There are some new employees who do not have the requisite knowledge and skills to perform a job. The training will aim to bring them up to speed.

❑ A new task has been defined, and no one in the company has the skills to perform it. The aim will be to train employees for this new function.

Other reasons can be related to job environment, policy issues or management issues. Since the needs assessment phase is really a consulting phase, the trainer must acquire all possible information to best define the training objectives.

At the end of this section, we provide a checklist of pertinent information to gather. However, first let us describe eight different techniques for information gathering.

Observation

Visit the workplace, the offices and the production lines, observing the way people behave and interact, and how the offices are arranged. You can also observe meetings, planning sessions and decision-making sessions.

Your observation does not have to be structured; just walking around can be enough. Observation can provide a lot of information about installations, machinery, behaviour and organizational structures. You can also notice things about the atmosphere of the company, the way people interact, their relationship to hierarchy. Do not walk around with a pad in your hand taking notes; you will be looked upon suspiciously. However, once outside, take notes of what you observed quickly before you forget.

Advantages	*Disadvantages*
• *It minimizes interruptions to the work flow.* • *It generates on-site data.* • *It is value-adding to the trainer, who will be able to speak about the participants' workplace during the course.*	• *It requires keen observation skills using knowledge of both content and process.* • *It may be perceived as spying.* • *If you do not know the industry, the information acquired may be very superficial.*

Questionnaires

Questionnaires can take the form of surveys or random polls, administered to a selection of employees from all levels in the organization, or to all employees, if there are not too many. You can use a variety of question formats: open ended, projective, forced choice or priority ranking. Questionnaires can be self-administered by mail or by e-mail under controlled or uncontrolled conditions. It is important to respect the confidentiality of the respondents when reporting back to management.

You will find that, although people are always curious to find out the results of questionnaires and surveys, they are often reluctant to spend time answering them. When a questionnaire is sent the entire staff of a firm a 50% response rate is typical. You need to explain in your introduction letter the purpose of the questionnaire and what you intend to do with the information. Confidentiality will of course be of paramount importance.

Advantages	*Disadvantages*
• *Can reach a large number of people in a short time and in an inexpensive manner.*	• *Questions need to be well thought out – constructing a good questionnaire can be time consuming.*
• *Allow people to express themselves without fear or embarrassment.*	• *Can be of little utility in ascertaining causes of problems or possible solutions.*
• *Questions can call for numerical answers and/or provide space for comments.*	• *Many questionnaires suffer low response rates.*
	• *Require extensive follow-up.*

Key consultation

Another way you can collect information is by meeting and consulting with key people in the company who, because of their position or their knowledge, can provide insight on what the training needs are.

These key people could be:

❑ Chairperson of the board;

❑ Head of a department;

❑ Individuals of a special service/area;

❑ Members of professional associations.

You will find that it is very important to select the right people for those key consultations. Unless the programme you are planning is of interest to him or her, you will rarely meet the chairperson. Quite likely, it will be a middle manager who has been put in charge of the training project. Sometimes a manager expresses a request for a training, delegates its organization and planning to a subordinate, and then intervenes at the end of the planning process with totally different ideas and opinions about what should be done. This can be very demoralizing. One way to avoid this is to have key consultations with the 'project sponsor' or the people concerned. In SMEs, however, you will often find that the owner of the company will be interested in meeting and discussing his or her views on the training objectives.

When deciding with whom to have these consultations, try to understand who are the parties concerned by the project and how training may affect them.

Advantages	*Disadvantages*
• *Relatively simple and inexpensive to conduct.*	• *Can be biased since they are based on subjective viewpoints: people tend to see training from their own individual or organizational perspective.*
• *Input can be solicited from individuals with different perspectives and from different disciplines.*	• *May give an incomplete picture.*

Print media

Print media can be an important source of information. News media, professional journals, in-house publications, and industry notes or trade magazines are all reliable sources of information. The interest of print media is to become more familiar with the industry as a whole, the positioning of the firm, the image it tries to project, what it wants to pay attention to, and so on.

Advantages

- *Can be an excellent source of information for uncovering and clarifying needs.*
- *Information that is current and in the public arena.*
- *It is readily available and is apt to have already been reviewed by the client group.*

Group discussions

Group discussions are similar to interviews (structured or unstructured, formal or informal) but they use the group as a means in itself. In interviews you gather the opinions of one individual. In group discussions, the opinions of all the members present will be confronted and challenged. Your facilitation skills will be put to the test.

The group will need to know from the outset what you are trying to achieve and what you will do with the information gathered. Even if they will not be further involved in the planning, you should thank them and inform them of the follow-up. Discussions tend to raise the level of expectations from people who participate, so you need to have a plan as to what will follow so that the process does not end in disappointment.

As in key consultation, you will need to gather the right combination of people around the table, so that they are representative of different opinions and experiences. You can use two approaches in composing a group:

❑ Choose a sample of the population that will be your future audience.

❑ Gather decision-makers who are key in the planning of the training.

There is a certain art in using the group to gather more information than you would through one-on-one interviews with each group member. There are many tools (feedback, reformulation, force field, mirroring) that you can use to structure the discussion. For a discussion of some process-consulting tools, see module 2.

Of course, a prerequisite for leading a good discussion is that you already be well informed about the company, its internal policies, dynamics and environment.

Advantages	*Disadvantages*
• *Allows quick, on-the-spot synthesis of a variety of viewpoints.* • *Engages the client more broadly in thinking about their needs and the ways to address them.*	• *Takes time away from people's jobs.* • *May be difficult to organize because of the number of participants (timing).* • *May deliver ambiguous data, because divergent views may be expressed.* • *Can be inhibiting if hierarchy is present.*

Tests

Tests provide a good insight into the technical level of the population you will target and can be administered without the trainer being present. They are useful tools if you intend to deliver technical skills training and need to target the course precisely to a specific level of skill or know-how.

You need to be transparent and reassure employees that the results of the test will not be used in any kind of performance assessment or evaluation.

Advantages	*Disadvantages*
• *Can help determine the cause of a problem related to a deficiency in knowledge or skills.* • *Results are easily quantifiable and comparable.*	• *Only few tests available already designed and validated for specific situations.* • *May be intimidating: employees may fear they are being assessed on their performance or for promotion purposes.*

Documents, records, reports

You can gather a lot of information from company documents such as annual reports, organizational charts, policy manuals, audits, budgets or minutes of meetings. You could also ask to consult employee records, monthly reports or programme evaluation studies: anything produced internally that can be read by an outsider. You will find that not every company is good at keeping minutes of meetings or of decision-making processes. Though you may gain valuable insight into how the company works, it is quite time-consuming to review a large quantity of documents.

Advantages	*Disadvantages*
• *Provide excellent insight into the workings of a company.* • *Can be collected with a minimum of effort without interrupting the work flow.*	• *Provide an insight into the past rather than the current situation.* • *Analytical skills may be required in order to assess some technical documents.* • *It is not always easy to have access to the right material.* • *Reading large amounts of documents is time-consuming*

Interviews

Interviews offer a large amount of flexibility thanks to the one-on-one format. They can be formal or casual, structured or unstructured. They may be held with a sample of a particular group (board, staff, committee) or with everyone concerned. You can conduct an interview by phone or in person, at work or away from the worksite.

It is difficult to perform an organizational analysis without at least some interviews. They allow you to obtain objective information but also perceptions and analysis of problems, difficulties and successes. Furthermore, face-to-face interviews can increase interest for the training project and can encourage people to buy in to the project.

Some interviews can be totally unstructured and left to the flow of the conversation, but it is much better to prepare a questionnaire or draft a series of questions in order to make the process more structured. You need to have researched the company or the industry in order to ask pertinent questions.

In interviews, as in all the other information-gathering methods, you need to emphasize that you will respect the anonymity of the respondent, as a matter of professional ethics.

As for a group discussion, interviewees need to be told what is the purpose of the interviews and what you will do with the information gathered. You need to let them know of the outcome of your work, even if it is just a simple letter describing the programme design. This is important, not least because your interaction with some members of staff and management is likely to make people curious and raise their expectations. With the help of your main contact in the company, you must manage these expectations and make sure the purpose of the exercise is clear.

You may need to interview the same person several times; the first meeting may be lengthier and the last one may be more focussed on expectations.

The final step, and the most difficult, is to synthesize your findings and incorporate them into your analysis.

Advantages	*Disadvantages*
• *Can be very good at revealing feelings, leading to causes of a problem.* • *Respondents may direct you to possible solutions.* • *Allow the client to represent himself spontaneously and on his or her own terms.*	• *Time-consuming.* • *Can be difficult to analyse and quantify, particularly if they follow an unstructured format.* • *It requires a certain skill to put people at ease, while still probing for what you need.* • *Once you have led interviews, the client will most probably expect a report – this is time-consuming to write and can be challenged.*

Here are simple principles to keep in mind when interviewing:

❑ Make sure you have access to a private space for the interview (for instance, in meeting room, rather than an open-plan office).

❑ Put your respondent at ease by using a relaxed conversational style.

❑ Assure your respondent of the confidentiality of the conversation. Yes, general results and analysis will be available to management or relevant personnel but no names and comments will be communicated.

❑ Treat your respondent with respect and tact, and don't be judgmental. The purpose of the interview is to elicit ideas and opinions, not change mentalities.

❑ Dress and act professionally, and in a way that is appropriate to the position of the interviewee.

❑ Ask questions in sequence. It is best if you mark them off on a sheet next to you.

❑ Take notes while the respondent speaks. Be sure to tell him or her that you will be taking notes and explain what you will do with them. The more transparent you are the less suspicious interviewees will be.

❑ Use open-ended questions. Probe and mirror what the interviewee has said to get confirmation.

❑ Use positive words of encouragement such as 'yes', 'good', 'I see', 'that is good information', etc.

❑ Don't let respondents criticize their colleagues or complain about the workplace; watch out for gossip.

Basic information to obtain

When a request has been expressed for a training programme to improve employees' performance, there are some basic items of information you need to obtain. The following can form the basis for your checklist.

The organization

❑ Goals of the organization as a whole;

❑ Methods by which the organization hopes to accomplish those goals;

❑ Values of the company/industry in general;

❑ Policies relevant to the function in question;

❑ Policies relevant to performance enhancement and training;

❑ Trends in the company as a whole;

❑ Trends in the organizational structure;

❑ Perceived performance-related problems within the organization.

The unit or department

❑ Management goals;

❑ Management values;

❑ Management written and unwritten policies;

❑ Attitudes of managers; their perceptions or actual and expected task performance levels;

❑ Trends in the target function, and those above and below it in the company structure;

❑ Policies on performance enhancement or training;

❑ Management attitudes toward training;

❑ Implicit and explicit expectations and attitudes of employees regarding their job, working environment, company as a whole, managers, peers, etc.

Performance

❑ Performance level which employees are capable of;

❑ Performance level at which employees are presently working;

❑ Performance level expected by management;

❑ Performance level expected by employees and peers;

❑ Performance level employees perceive that they could conceivably attain, and circumstances that would result in those levels;

❑ Factors which employees and managers feel interfere with performance (physical, political, environmental, etc.).

Methods for collecting information

Document analysis

❑ Organizational statements of mission and long-range goals;

❑ Organizational policies and procedures;

❑ Budgets;

❑ Productivity reports;

❑ Performance appraisal;

❑ Annual reports;

❑ Financial reports;

❑ Annual reviews;

❑ Schedules;

❑ Training materials.

Interviews and questionnaires

❑ Upper management;

❑ Unit management;

❑ Work groups;

❑ Individual employee;

❑ Professional associations.

Observation of employees

❑ Observation of employees who are performing below level;

❑ Observation of experts.

Observation/analysis of physical or social environment

Written tests or performance tests of knowledge and skills

Defining training objectives

'The secret of success is constancy of purpose.'
Benjamin Disraeli

The purpose of training is to take a group of adults from an initial situation, an initial level of knowledge, know-how and behaviour, and bring them to a new level. In order to choose the means for arriving at this new level, you must first situate it precisely and accurately.

Defining training objectives allows you to:

❑ Determine the direction of the course, what new knowledge and new know-how that the participants will have at the end of the training.

❑ Choose the most appropriate facilitation process.

❑ Check with participants and their employers whether the programme is relevant to their needs.

❑ Help participants mentally prepare for the training (they know what to expect).

❑ Readjust the process while the training is going on or at the end of the training if it has to be repeated.

❑ Verify that objectives have been reached.

❑ Facilitate the evaluation process so the actual results of the training can be measured against the objectives.

In order to define training objectives, you have to place yourself in the position of the participants. Too often, objectives are defined in terms of intentions (what the trainer intends to do), or in terms of content (what the subject matter will be). This misunderstanding of the meaning of objective leads to faulty definitions of the type:

❑ I (the trainer) will make them aware of ...

❑ I will make them understand ...

❑ I will explain ...

❑ I will provide this information ...

❑ I will cover the following topics ...

In fact the objective should answer one key question only: What will participants gain? What new behaviour, skill or knowledge will they acquire?

We can distinguish three types of objectives:

❑ *Cognitive* objectives, or knowledge;

❑ *Psychometric* objectives, or know-how, skills and competencies;

❑ *Affective* objectives, or attitudes and behaviours.

These objectives are defined in terms of 'being able to ...' followed by a verb. Here is a list of verbs that could meet one of the three objectives:

Cognitive (knowledge)	*Psychometric (skills)*	*Affective (behaviour)*
Know	*Repair*	*Adjust or adapt*
Understand	*Control*	*Feel*
Define	*Use*	*Demystify*
Specify	*Act*	*Integrate*
Retain	*Do*	*Motivate*
Name	*Change*	
Identify	*Read*	
Memorize	*Interpret*	
Explain	*Draft*	
Plan		

All training, whether technical, theoretical or behavioural will contain the types of objectives that we have identified above and in the progression of the course (the design session by session) will take into account one of them at a time. You need to make sure objectives include some from at least two categories or more (generally knowledge and skills).

Two simple models will help you draft programme objectives. The SMART model stipulates that programme objectives have to be:

S = Specific
M = Measurable
A = Attainable
R = Realistic
T = Time bound

(T can also stand for Tractable, meaning easy to monitor; or for Truthful, meaning objectives that you, the trainer, can seriously commit to.)

Another model for objective-setting criteria goes by the acronym SPIRO:

S = Specific: objectives specify exactly what we are going to do;

P = Performance: focus on high value results, not on activities;

I = Involvement: participants need to be involved in setting the objectives;

R = Realism: objectives need to be realistic;

O = Observable: the achievement of the objectives should be tangible and measurable.

Once the global objectives of the programme have been defined, we then need to list the sub-objectives (or intermediary objectives), which set the progression of the course.

The construction of a training programme consists in identifying the steps that the participants will have to go through in order to reach the final objective. Each session will have its objective (session objective) clearly defined so that the sum of the parts will create the whole. Figure 10 shows how the intermediary steps build up to the final objective.

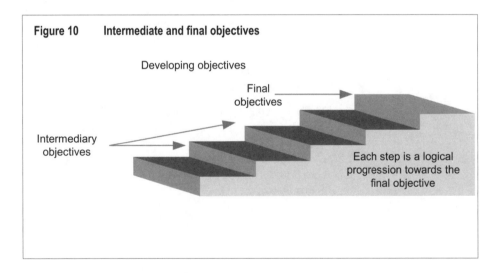

Figure 10   Intermediate and final objectives

Developing objectives

Final objectives

Intermediary objectives

Each step is a logical progression towards the final objective

❑ You must walk on each step, and one at a time;

❑ Steps are not interchangeable;

❑ The height of the steps depends on the capacity of the participants;

❑ The pace at which you climb the steps depends on the time at your disposal, and the time that trainees need to reach the objective of each step.

Choosing teaching methods

Teaching methods

Choosing a teaching method is, as we have seen, motivated by the need to stimulate the participants' interest, make sure they understand, and maximize the chances of internalizing.

Training methods can be classified into three broad categories:

❑ *Affirmative methods* (or presentation methods): lectures, forums, panels, presentations, demonstrations, audio-visual presentations.

❑ *Interactive methods:* brainstorming, group discussions, role-playing, simulations.

❑ *Exploratory methods:* case studies, exercises.

Lecturing is traditionally the most common and frequently used method, probably because it is the one most people are familiar with from school. Lecturing implies an active role for the trainer and a passive role for the participant. Although less common, interactive and exploratory methods work well with adult learners because they solicit their input and are in many ways more effective in teaching skills and behaviours.

Which method to choose?

The selection of one or several teaching method depends on several factors, which are listed below (though not in order of priority).

❑ *The expectations of the trainees and their motivations.* What would they like to know at the end of the training, what will be useful to them?

❑ *The learning habits of the participants.* In some cultures people view the trainer as the expert, like a professor. These learners will favour expository methods, such as lectures and reading. They may react negatively to interactive methods. It is important to be receptive to such expectations but also to 'stretch' the learners by using unfamiliar tools, like case studies, videos, or group work.

❑ *The company culture.* This differs widely and influences the way people will interact with other trainees and with the trainer. You could have employees of all levels, and if the culture is very hierarchical, subordinates might find difficult to talk in front of superiors and vice versa.

❑ *The size of the group.* The number of participants has an impact on the level of participation you can expect. Small audiences allow for all interactive methods (active, creative, and demonstrative), while with bigger groups, you might want to use more 'static' tools, unless you have more than one trainer. As a rule of thumb, for interactive methods the ratio of 1 trainer for 15–18 participants is adequate.

❑ *The level of knowledge of the participants.* Their level of expertise, experience and academic background influences how they will learn. For instance, a person with a lot of experience but little academic background may quickly tune out of theoretical lectures. Conversely, academically minded participants will have high expectations regarding the quality of the presentation and models delivered.

❑ *The time frame.* Lectures and demonstrations are comparatively less time consuming than interactive methods. Indeed, it takes time to organize group work, brief the participants, form groups, facilitate discussions, listen to them report back. There is a tendency to underestimate time needed for interactive methods.

❑ *The subject matter.* For instance, when trying to impart technical knowledge, such as operating a machine or implementing new procedures, it is best to demonstrate and involve participants in practice, rather than just delivering lectures.

❑ *The trainer.* His or her habits, communicative and logistical abilities influence the choice of tools and methods. Some trainers are good at presentation but do not know how to handle audience participation, while others may be poor presenters but good facilitators. The programme might require adjustments to take into consideration those preferences.

Using different methods dynamically

Alternating different methods, according to the circumstances outlined above, has another benefit: it gives the course a dynamic rhythm, and avoids boredom. In fact methods should also be alternated to meet the objectives of the trainer, as illustrated in figure 11:

❑ Get them interested, get their attention;

❑ Make sure that participants understand and integrate new ideas or skills;

❑ Make sure that they have retained and assimilated the new ideas or skills.

Each of the tasks requires a different method and teaching tool. For example, a group activity may stimulate interest in the subject, while a presentation and a video may increase understanding. As long as the choice of an activity is clear (and made clear to the trainees), you can use any format you want.

It is important to avoid monotony by varying the sequence (for example, do not always present the theory and then move on to doing exercises to increase understanding, and finish by a test to ensure retention). You should instead strive to make the course as varied and lively as possible.

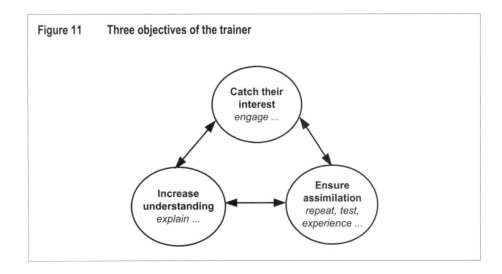

Figure 11   Three objectives of the trainer

Quite naturally, the content of the course tends to increase in complexity as the hours go by. Most of the time, interest decreases while complexity increases. You will have noticed audiences that disconnect as soon as the content becomes more sophisticated. In fact the interest of the trainees is directly related to both time and difficulty, rendering some portion of most training programme time ineffective (see figure 12).

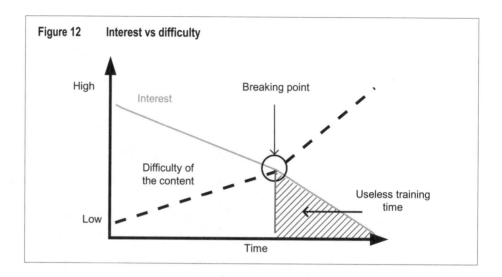

To avoid this pitfall, you should use motivating methods which sustain the participants' interest while the difficulty increases. Maintaining a balance between interest (motivation) and complexity becomes the challenge of a good training design. The result is a positive correlation between increasing difficulty and trainee interest, as shown in figure 13.

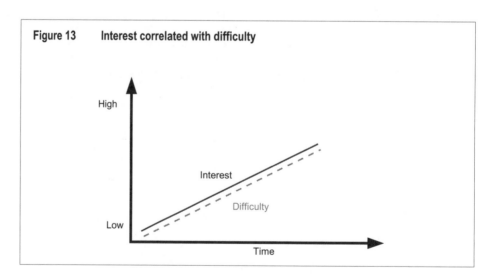

How do we memorize?

Just as the trainer needs to constantly question the adequacy of a teaching tool for a specific subject, he or she also needs to keep in mind how participants learn best (see the discussion in module 1 on learning styles).

All the research that has been done on memorization has come up with similar results. As figure 14 shows, we memorize and internalize knowledge through reinforcement from several different senses. Thus the more participants 'do', are involved, and realize what they do by talking about it and explaining it, the more they will remember. In fact, what this tells us about adult learners is that group activities are an excellent method because it requires them to 'see', 'listen', 'say' and 'do'.

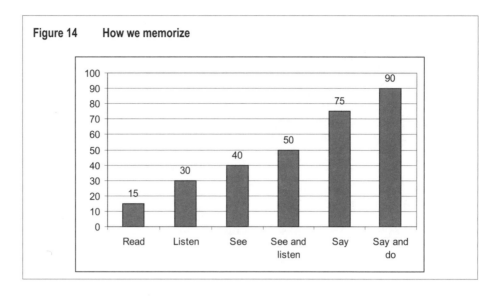

Figure 14   How we memorize

Choosing your format

Once you have analysed the training needs, determined the objectives, and specified the audience, the training programme itself will need to be designed. A first step to this design is to choose the format. Several forms of delivery fall into the categories of training. The choice of one or the other depends on the size of the group, the time frame and the teaching objectives.

Conference or convention

A conference or convention brings together a large audience, often from more than one company, to listen to lectures or presentations by invited speakers or members of the audience. The purpose of a conference is usually to present a new product, a new strategy, or to convey a very structured message. Conferences can last one day or several. They can be accompanied by large quantitites of audio-visual information. Care should be given to the communication supports: logos, posters, banners, press conferences, handouts, and events during which participants can socialize and network. Because of their size, conferences or conventions aim only at transferring information and knowledge.

Colloquium or symposium

A colloquium gathers specialists to discuss a specific issue, through lectures or panels presented by participants. It is a forum for discussion and debate of new concepts and ideas. The objective is often scientific, and this is why the term is mostly used in an academic context. However, you find such events in industry, with cross-industry functional meetings, such as a human resources management symposium, where the aim is to network, but also to benchmark and discover what is new in the field.

Seminar

The seminar brings together a small group of learners under the leadership of a teacher or trainer, for an intensive course of study. Because of its academic ring, the term is often reserved for courses with a high theoretical content, aimed more at highly skilled employees or high-level managers.

Workshop

A workshop implies a small number of participants, like a seminar, but the emphasis is on interaction and exchange of information among them. A workshop can be the venue for finding operational solutions to practical problems for instance. However, the term is loosely used, and like a seminar, a workshop can describe any training programme where you acquire skills, or learn about a field under the teaching of one of several trainers or specialists.

Course

The most general term of all, a course can take place over several weeks or even months, covering a subject extensively, under the teaching of one or several professors or specialists.

On-the-job training

On the job training is a course delivered at the workplace or under simulated conditions. Sometimes, this is a section of a classroom-based course that takes place in the workplace or in a laboratory environment. It can include coaching and advisory inputs, and is aimed at developing professional skills, expertise and knowledge.

Open learning

Any training course that takes place outside of the classroom or a traditional training environment, in the learner's own time and at his or her chosen pace is known as open learning. Open learning courses are offered by correspondence, and usually involve self-study with occasional short workshops. They can be supported by videos, audiotapes or written materials (course book, self-testing exercises).

E-learning

Web-based open learning is known as e-learning. The use of the Internet permits more interactive teaching methods and practices than the traditional open learning format, such as audio and video, instant messaging debates with other participants or course facilitator, electronic self-testing tools, etc. However, e-learning lacks one essential catalyst for learning: human interaction and stimulus. It is unlikely therefore to ever replace 'live' training, but remains a useful component.

Coaching

One-on-one training or counselling is known as coaching. A trainer or a facilitator works with one or several employees individually in order to achieve personal development, behavioural or attitudinal objectives. The emphasis is on close cooperation between trainer and trainee. Coaching takes place in the workplace (in a private space) or outside, for a predetermined number of sessions. Objectives are set by agreement between the boss, the trainee and the trainer. The objectives are clear from the outset and communicated to all parties concerned. Because coaching is a very expensive form of training, it must be based on clear objectives that meet specific expectations from the employer. The result of the coaching session can be a decision to further develop the trainee's skills and knowledge through more training (course, seminar, etc.).

Some coaching may also address teams or groups, for example, by helping teams improve the way they operate during meetings or decision-making processes. In this case, the facilitator observes the real work situation and, jointly with the team, defines the improvement areas and highlights potential avenues for progress.

Main focus of training objectives	Most suitable types of training events
Changes in attitudes	Conference, senior level seminar
Knowledge acquisition	Course, seminar, open learning, study tours abroad
Skills acquisition	Workshop, on-the-job training
Any two or all three of the above	Seminar, course

Source: *Handbook for Trainers in International Purchasing and Supply Management*, ITC, 1996, page 26.

Building your programme

Now that you have understood the needs, targeted your audience, set your objectives and decided in what format to deliver the training, you need to build your programme. As Disraeli said, 'The secret of success is constancy of purpose': you will need to constantly keep in mind why you are doing each activity at every step of the training process.

The factors that are to be taken in consideration for building a programme have been defined: they are the participants, the time, the subject, and the tools. Module 4 will present a palette of tools from which you can choose. The art of programme design is to blend all of those elements into a whole.

Building the training programme means proceeding step by step towards the training objective, that is, the acquisition or change of skills, knowledge, behaviours or attitudes. You will break the objectives into units that can be called 'modules' or 'sessions'. Each session will require an objective, one or several teaching tools and a time frame.

In between those content-bearing sessions you will plan for breaks: coffee breaks, lunch or dinner, and recreational or reflection time.

❑ One- or two-day workshops or seminars should have a coffee break in the morning, one in the afternoon and a lunch.

❑ A three-day workshop should be interrupted at some point by several hours of break (activity or free time) in order to refresh and remotivate the participants.

❑ A four-day workshop definitely requires time off for reflection, a site visit, a recreational event or just an afternoon off.

You will also need to vary the setting in which learning is taking place: plenary, group work, individual work, audiovisual work or experiential activities.

On a blank page, write your objectives first (you may use the mind-mapping tool described in module 4). Then break this into sub-objectives, which will become the objective of each session. Associate with each session objective the key content, the concepts, the models or the methods the participants will have to acquire. It is best to alternate acquisition of knowledge, appropriation of the knowledge, and the practice of the skills or new behaviour.

We suggest you follow the following format for building your programme. Using spreadsheet or word processing software, set an A4 sheet to landscape format and create seven columns as shown in table 10.

Table 10	Programme planning grid					
Session	**Time**	**Objective**	**Content**	**Tool**	**Material**	**Logistics**
Session 1						
Session 2						
Session 3						

Time is pretty much limited by the biological needs of the human body and the human mind. It is inconceivable to consider two hours of work without a break. It is best to plan for a break every 90 minutes. You need to assess realistically whether the time allocated is sufficient. You can do so once you have provided the objectives and content. The easy way out is to ask yourself what can be done in 90 minutes and define objectives accordingly. However, we recommend that you start instead with your objectives and your content and then decide how much time you need.

Objectives are assigned to each step of the process, using the SMART or SPIRO methods described earlier in this module. You may also select the tools you will use to verify whether objectives have been met.

Content describes the ideas, skills, know-how that you will deliver. What do you need participants to understand, learn, remember, compare, master?

Tools are the teaching methods you will use. Some of these were outlined above; more will be discussed in module 4. The purpose of the tools is to communicate, and help learners assimilate the content.

Materials are anything you use in the course, such as handouts, overheads, support documentation, presentations and worksheets. Preparing good materials is time consuming but worth the effort, because they are what participants will take home with them. Materials should be professional, well produced, appealing but not necessarily glossy. There should be uniformity in their format, and all sources and references should be quoted. (More tips on organizing handouts and materials will be provided in module 6.)

Logistics refers to whatever practical details need to be organized in order for the course to take place. (This is discussed in detail in module 6.)

If you are running the programme with more than one trainer, add another column, 'responsibility', for who is responsible for each item.

Writing a training offer

Writing a training offer is a major step in selling your training service. You may write an offer in response to a specific request, or send an unsolicited offer, or sales pitch, for a course you have designed. These two possibilities require different approaches, which are outlined below.

Writing an offer in response to a specific request

When responding to a training request, your proposal is structured very much like the consulting proposal that was described in module 2.

❑ In the first part you will reformulate what you have seen, understood or have been asked to do.

❑ In the second part, you will outline your analysis of the situation and make recommendations.

❑ In the third part, you will make your detailed offer (content, structure, logistics, financial terms, etc.).

The proposal is a 'calling card' for your services – you want to make as good an impression as possible. It should be self-contained, because you may not have a chance to explain it by phone or in a meeting. Do spend time writing your proposal, because you may be competing with other companies in a bidding process. Often it is the best-written proposal that will be selected, all other factors being equal (expertise, price). Although this is not always the case, you want to put all the chances on your side.

Depending on the subject matter and the complexity of the request, a training offer or proposal can be from three to more than twenty pages long. A full training package for a company involving many different competency-building courses would be even longer. The documents should be as exhaustive as possible since the potential buyer may collect offers until a certain date and then gather a committee to shortlist two or three offers. The selection committee may then decide to pursue extensive interviews with the shortlisted vendors before making their final selection.

Since proposal writing was discussed in detail in module 2, we will simply remind you briefly of the elements a proposal should include:

Title page

❑ Title of the programme;

❑ Name of your contact;

❑ Client's company name and address, and their logo if available;

❑ Trainer's name, company and address;

❑ Date.

Understanding of the situation (as presented by the client)

Summarize the request for training as the client presented it to you. Make sure you use similar language, repeat the stated concerns, the examples given and the purpose of the request.

Your analysis of the situation

Here you should provide an analysis of the situation as you see it. This sometimes means going beyond what the client really wants. It is an in-depth analysis that demonstrates that you have spent time reflecting on the situation. If you question the request because you feel it is inappropriate or does not meet a real need, you may say so at this point. You may also provide a second option if you think it is more appropriate and you can provide the service.

In this section, you can also identify some critical success factors for ensuring that the training be as productive as possible. In fact, training is only part of a holistic process. If an organization needs to change, or if new procedures are introduced, their success is dependent on other changes being implemented at the same time. It is your role as a trainer/consultant to provide the big picture and define the critical elements that need to be put in place simultaneously for the training effort to be productive.

The proposal

This outlines the proposed training that you will provide. It should state, with details:

❑ Name of the programme;

❑ Time frame;

❑ Target audience;

❑ Overall objectives;

❑ Detailed agenda (split into sessions with main points covered in each session).

In some cases you may want to provide two options for the client to choose from. If this is so, you should also state the advantages and disadvantages of each option, so that the client can choose the one that best meets his or her needs.

Other considerations

If there are any special needs for the programme you should state them. For instance, some programmes require pre-workshop preparation or a selection process. If you recommend that the programme be delivered away from the company and accommodation will be required, specify why. Provide all guidance on how to implement the project.

Critical success factors

In this section you describe the responsibilities of the client and that steps that must be taken to ensure the success of the project. Sometimes the critical success factor is simply the dedication shown by top management or middle management to the project, and the way they communicate this to employees, suppliers and distributors. You need to state your expectations clearly.

Schedules and timeline

Here you will write a timeline describing what needs to happen when, in order to make sure the programme is delivered on time. This planning may concern not only the company that is buying the programme, but also the communication process between the client company and the training company. The schedule will include:

❑ Submission dates of full programme design;

❑ Dates for selection of participants;

❑ Submission dates for programme materials.

Logistics

Logistical issues include dates, location, equipment, meals, and other resources, as well as production and distribution of training materials and the sequence of delivery, if there are several programmes.

Financial terms

This is where you will provide the financial terms for your training services. They should be as detailed as possible. We recommend that you itemize the services in such a way that the client can gain a good idea what the final price is going to be. When a programme is tailor-made for a client, you can charge for preparation time.

There are different pricing methods:

❑ Price per participant;

❑ Price per session;

❑ Price per trainer;

❑ Flat fee (all inclusive itemized price).

The price should include materials unless you want to charge separately for proprietary tools or simulations.

Travel and living expenses are also charged to the client and should be estimated in the terms. They are, however, paid separately upon submission of receipts. It is important to put a cap on those expenses when they constitute an important part of the budget.

Don't forget to clearly state the currency and the terms of payment (time, whether cheque or wire transfer, etc.).

There are several possibilities for timing payment. Sometimes trainers are paid in several instalments, with a portion being paid up front, a portion halfway through and the final balance on completion. Sometimes the entire fee is paid after the end of the service. The advantage of requiring a partial payment up front is that it gives the client an incentive to maintain its commitment.

Specify whether you need a purchase order or a contract. If you want a contract you need to define who should draft the contract.

Writing an unsolicited offer

If you are writing to a prospective client to offer your services, you are essentially advertising. The objective of your letter or presentation leaflet will be to communicate, as succinctly as possible, the main advantages of your training service. These 11 points should serve as a guideline for what to include in your presentation leaflet.

❑ **Programme name:** a clear and descriptive title.

❑ **The story:** a short paragraph that explaining the course subject matter and how it is relevant to a specific profession, type of company, industry, etc. The story should be appealing and include some concrete examples.

❑ **The target audience:** specify who would most benefit from the training or who should think about sending their employees to the course, and why. You can also describe your target audience in looser terms focusing on objectives. Are you involved in this type of situation? Do you face the following difficulties? Do you need to improve your performance in the following area?

❑ **The objectives:** should be described in terms of what knowledge and competencies the participants will acquire through the training. Those objectives should be listed in bullet points, always from the point of view of the learner.

❑ **Expected outcomes:** some trainers like to differentiate between the objectives and the outcomes. The outcome describes what success looks like at the end of the training, when the new skills have been applied. Although you may differentiate the two, you can also write your objectives so that they are formulated as outcomes.

❑ **Content:** list briefly the different topics of the programme and provide examples of some of the methodologies which will be used (if they are of particular interest). This is not a full agenda, only a list of the main topics.

❑ **Logistics:** practical information about where the training will be held, whether it is residential or not, hours, venues, and how to get to them.

❑ **Cost:** simple information on price and terms of payment. Include a payment slip and date for final payment if necessary.

❑ **Trainers' credentials:** you may want to provide a short biography of the trainers, highlighting their credentials, experience and any details that will increase the credibility of the training. If you have guest speakers, mention them as well.

❑ **Pre-enrolment preparation:** if there are prerequisites for attending the course (a basic understanding of accounting for instance) you should mention them. You may also require participants to give you some information by filling out a questionnaire. If there is a pre-course assignment, give an idea of how long it will be (for example, three hours for reading course materials or preparing a presentation).

❑ **Other practical information:** could include application deadline, address and person to contact for additional information.

Module 4

Tools for trainers

Background

As a trainer you will have at your disposal a wide range of teaching tools. These consist of a variety of methods, techniques and instruments, as well as tips and tricks, which facilitate the learning process. As we have seen, the combination of different tools solicits in the learner different senses and styles of learning, which increases the likelihood that they will retain what they learn (see module 1 on learning styles, and module 3 on how we memorize). In contrast, learners retain on average only 10% of the content of a lecture.

In module 3 we discussed the factors that would lead you to choose one method or tool versus another at different stages in the programme. These include group size, time constraints, subject matter, the learning environment, and learning habits and knowledge level of the participants. These are some basic principles to follow when selecting the tools you will use with the group:

- ❑ Find a balance between affective, behavioural and cognitive learning;
- ❑ Vary methods and tools;
- ❑ Generate audience participation;
- ❑ Use the group to stimulate learning;
- ❑ Call on participants' expertise;
- ❑ Reformulate and repeat learned concepts and skills;
- ❑ Take any opportunity for real-life problem solving;
- ❑ Consider how participants will put learning into practice.

Let us look at each of these principles in a little more detail, before defining and discussing the advantages and disadvantages of a selection of tools.

Find a balance between affective, behavioural and cognitive learning. This implies that you vary your teaching style. For cognitive learning you will use lectures, documents, research, summaries. For behavioural learning you will use role-play and simulation. For affective learning you provide feedback and facilitation of new approaches through group dynamics.

Vary methods and tools. As you are well aware, people learn differently: some learn by reading, others by hearing, observing or doing. Make sure your choice of tools appeals to all these styles.

Generate audience participation. You do this by asking questions and challenging the audience. You can also ask the group to generate questions. The most effective way to do so is to create small discussion groups. Ask them to reflect on your presentation and to prepare questions that will deepen their understanding. This helps overcome participants' reluctance to speak up in front of the whole group. Sometimes, instead of providing the answers yourself, you can redirect the questions to your trainees ('That was a good question. Can anyone answer that?').

Use the group to stimulate learning. The variety of knowledge, experience and learning styles makes the group your most powerful learning tool. The group stimulates participants, while providing both support and emulation. 'Two heads are better than one' goes the saying: people working alone produce far less than three or four combined. You can organize learning groups, reading groups or project groups. When analysing situations or concepts, create sub-groups and ask them to reflect and report back in plenary. It is very stimulating for participants to present in front of their peers.

Call on participants' expertise. You should always know the profile of your trainees, their experience and the function they hold. Do not hesitate to address them as equals by appealing to their expertise, for instance by redirecting questions to them.

Reformulate and repeat learned concepts and skills. Say what you have to say, repeat what you have said, and summarize what you have said. Use all sorts of formats to do so: visual, verbal, texts, quotes, examples, illustrations and so on.

Take any opportunity for real-life problem solving. The more you can apply your teaching to real-life examples, the better you will be heard. Liven up your presentations with concrete examples, using videos, photographs, newspaper articles, or case studies that people can connect to.

Consider how participants will put learning into practice. Always make sure you explain the application and relevance of what you teach to the workplace, based on what you know of the participants' job descriptions and industries.

Tools described in this module

Forms of delivery

❏ Lectures.

❏ Panels.

❏ Guided teaching.

❏ Demonstrations.

Tools to stimulate discussion/refine understanding

❏ Affinity diagramming.

❏ Mind mapping.

❏ Brainstorming.

❏ Case studies.

Tools to create active participation and engagement

❏ Role-play.

❏ Simulation.

❏ Experiential learning exercises.

One on one

❏ Clinic.

❏ Psychometric instruments.

Hands-on

❏ Field trip.

Lectures

Lecturing is the most common and lowest-cost method for communicating general information to an audience, particularly a large one. For 15 minutes to an hour, the trainer speaks in front of a silent audience, whose only involvement is taking notes and perhaps asking questions for clarification.

Lectures are useful to introduce topics and get basic information across, but a pure lecture course will engage participants only intellectually. However, lectures need not be long: the lecturette, lasting 10 to 15 minutes is a good way to introduce new topics before moving on to more participative methods.

Module 5 discusses the practicalities of preparing and delivering lectures in more detail.

Use

❑ To give an overview a topic.

❑ To extensively discuss the theory or background of a topic.

Advantages

❑ Deliver a lot of information in a short period of time.

❑ Cost effective.

❑ Practical with very big groups.

❑ 'Lecturettes' can stimulate interest and are lighter than formal lengthy presentations.

Disadvantages

❑ Audience is passive.

❑ Participants may miss information if they do not take good notes (handouts may resolve this issue).

❑ Boredom: attention wavers after 20 minutes.

Group size

❑ Any.

Time

❑ No more than one hour – and don't plan a long lecture right after lunch!

Logistics

❑ Microphone for large audiences.

❑ Overhead projector.

❑ Video projector.

Preparation

❑ Prepare lecture on A5 cards.

❑ Use visuals to present the outline of the subject (and refer to it as you progress).

❑ Write up on the flip chart or whiteboard any new terminology, acronyms, figures that you quote in the lecture.

❑ If you want to encourage some audience participation prepare some questions to ask them at the end of the lecture.

❑ Prepare handouts.

Panels

A panel is a lecture format that brings together a group of experts to make a brief presentation on a specific subject and then debate their ideas and respond to questions from the audience. The panel discussion is facilitated by a moderator. Panel members ideally have varied expertise or contrasting opinions. This format is rewarding for an audience because it allows discussion and provides opinions and professional expertise that differ from the trainer's own. It is an added bonus if the panel members are well known in their field.

After an introduction by the trainer or the host acknowledging the presence of experts and presenting the purpose of the panel, each speaker makes a presentation. After each presentation, a few minutes are reserved for clarification or questions. After all the experts have spoken, you may open the debate, field questions from the audience and confront the variety of opinions that are represented in the panel. The one precondition for a lively panel session is that the audience participate; to do so they need to be familiar with the subject.

Use

❑ To confront different views on an issue.

❑ To push discussion of an issue to a higher level.

Advantages

❑ Stimulate participants by letting them interact with and meet experts.

❑ Expose them to contrasting views and opinions.

❑ Increase their understanding of a complex subject.

❑ Place participants and experts on the same level.

Disadvantages

❑ Access to experts can be difficult.

❑ Can be expensive to organize: panel members will expect their travel expenses to be paid, and may charge a fee for their participation.

❑ Unless the audience is well prepared, discussion can lag.

❑ Experts do not always deliver good presentations; sometimes they rely on their knowledge rather than preparing a structured speech, or use jargon that is too complex for the audience. It is, therefore, a good idea to vet presentations in advance.

❑ Panels are difficult to moderate. It requires some experience of facilitation to keep a panel from turning into just a series of short lectures.

Group size

❑ Any.

Time

❑ One hour is probably a minimum; 90 minutes is more realistic. The presentations should take up no more than half the allotted time.

Logistics

❑ Panel members should be visible. A stage is ideal.

❑ Microphone so that audience can hear.

❑ Other equipment as needed: overhead projector, video projector, etc. Check needs of panel members beforehand.

Preparation

❑ Select experts so that a variety of views are presented.

❑ Review content of presentation with each expert. Don't be embarrassed to request this, as the outcome of the panel will depend on it. Inform the experts of the content of the other presentations in order to avoid repetition.

❑ Prepare a short biography on each panel member.

❑ Prepare the text of your opening speech.

❑ Clearly define the focus of the panel and the expected outcome.

❑ Prepare two or three questions with which to start off the discussion in case the audience is too shy at first to ask questions. Prepare at least one polemical question that might get the experts to express diverging opinions.

❑ Write a thank you speech.

Guided teaching

Guided teaching is a way of leading the learner to answers by questioning, rather than providing the answers in a lecture. There are several methods you can use.

The first one is to put a question to the group and tap into the knowledge of participants. As participants answer, record what they say succinctly on a flip chart or whiteboard. You then compare their input with the lecture points you have in mind.

The second method is to distribute documents, articles, and research papers to the participants, to read before the next class. In class, put one or several questions to the group, record their answer on the whiteboard and then compare their input with the points you had in mind. Thanks to the preparation, their answers will be better informed than if they had relied only on prior knowledge.

Use

❑ To demystify a new subject: people realize they already know something about it.

❑ To check how much participants know about a subject.

❑ To consolidate knowledge.

Advantages

❑ Participative.

❑ Taps into know-how of participants: validating.

❑ Consolidates knowledge: people remember what they say.

❑ Encourages discovery.

Disadvantages

❑ Lack of participation is a big risk. It may be hard to get answers, or only a few of the more knowledgeable members of the group may respond while the rest remain silent.

❑ It takes quite a bit of skill to summarize participants' contributions and integrate them on the fly into the points you were planning to make.

❑ You may wish to finish with a lecturette, so have something ready if their contribution is not so rich.

Group size

Small to medium (you need to be able to call on everyone at least once).

Time

❑ 30–60 minutes.

Logistics

❑ Whiteboard, blackboard, flip chart.

Preparation

❑ If you ask the trainees to prepare for the session by reading, gather a broad variety of material on the subject.

❑ Prepare your questions thoroughly and write them on the board.

Demonstration

Instead of giving a lecture on a procedure or process you may be able to use a demonstration. This involves walking your audience through the actual steps of the process; it is showing by doing. Instead of describing the procedure of changing a light bulb, for instance, you get a ladder and a light bulb, climb on the ladder and screw the bulb into the socket, explaining each step as you do it. Involving the participants in the demonstration is important: they need not only to hear and see, but also to do.

You could demonstrate how to fill in customs documents, report cash flow, answer questionnaires, verify the quality of a product, repair a machine, and so on. For this you need to provide the group with the document, product or machine. Always start the demonstration from the big picture, providing a framework to work with, and then break it into steps. Move onto the next step only when the previous one has been performed and understood correctly.

Use

❑ To train participants in performing a procedure or set of actions.

Advantages

❑ Hands-on, concrete and clear.

❑ By making participants do it themselves you can check whether they have understood.

❑ Participative.

Disadvantages

❑ The trainer needs to know the procedure very well.

❑ Time-consuming.

❑ You need to have enough samples of the item you are demonstrating. If it is a machine you may have only one; in this case you will need to break the audience into small groups, so that everyone can see your demonstration, and the procedure can then be performed by each. You will need to find other activities for the rest of the group to do in the meantime.

Group size

❑ Small.

Time

❑ 30–60 minutes. Practice can take longer.

Logistics

❏ Provide enough materials (documents, product, machines, etc.) for practice.

❏ Overhead projector is essential if demonstrating how to do a paper-based procedure.

Preparation

❏ Break the procedure into steps. This is not always easy. Find a way to wrap things up at the end.

❏ Practice the demonstration before delivering it.

❏ Have participants practice after you have done your demonstration. You may need to write a case so that they can apply the demonstration to a real-life situation.

❏ Prepare a list of frequently asked questions in order to anticipate the questions trainees may have.

❏ Have a lot of lively examples ready to illustrate the purpose of the procedure.

Brainstorming

Brainstorming is a basic technique for launching a discussion. The purpose of brainstorming is to generate a whole range of ideas, suggestions or solutions to a stated question or problem. These will range from the obvious to the complex or even the absurd – nothing is rejected at first.

To avoid it becoming a free-for-all, the brainstorming should follow a specific sequence:

❏ **Data dumping:** a large quantity of ideas are generated, and written down without being judged.

❏ **Clarification:** all ideas listed are made clear to everyone.

❏ **Evaluation:** through discussion the merits of different ideas are compared.

❏ **Prioritization:** the most useful and important ideas are selected.

The first phase is the easiest: ideas are jotted down on the board as they pop out of people's minds no matter how absurd they may seem. The key to a fruitful brainstorming is then to channel these ideas through dialogue and discussion, so as to hone in on the most relevant ideas and then build upon them.

Brainstorming can be led by the trainer for a small group, or can be put into practice in a larger group by splitting it into small groups, each of which will brainstorm together and then present their conclusions to the entire group. Small groups need to appoint one of their members as a facilitator.

Affinity diagramming and mind mapping, discussed next, are based on the same principles, but use a somewhat different format.

Use

❏ To generate ideas and foster creative, 'out-of-the-box' thinking.

Advantages

❏ Encourages creative thinking.

❏ Taps into diversity of experience and expertise in a group.

❏ Participants are active and involved.

Disadvantages

❑ Takes time to sift through a large number of ideas and discuss each of them.

❑ Can be hard to get started in small groups: someone in the group has to volunteer to lead, and the group has to understand the process well. Often groups end up discussing the validity of an idea rather than just generating them. You should remind them to avoid making judgements in the first phase.

Group size

❑ Small group or large group divided into sub-groups of three to five people.

Time

❑ About 30 minutes.

Logistics

❑ Flip chart.

Preparation

❑ Review with the groups the steps and principles of brainstorming.

❑ Agree on a clear description of the problem or situation.

❑ Get each sub-group to appoint a facilitator.

Affinity diagramming

Originally developed as a process-consulting tool, the affinity diagram is useful for identifying the various components of a complex process or project and organizing them in a logical way. Its advantage is that it forces groups to produce a lot of ideas and suggestions without launching into a discussion.

Affinity diagramming starts off like a brainstorming exercise. Individually, participants list their ideas and write each on a Post-it note, using the brainstorming technique. Post-its are stuck to the wall and are then organized in broad categories, by regrouping them into clusters of similar ideas (Post-its can be moved around easily, allowing you to try out different groupings). Each cluster is then organized: redundant ideas are eliminated, alternative ideas are kept.

Once all ideas or suggestions are organized, the affinity diagramming is finished. The result is an organized list of ideas that the group can work on. The next step of the project could be to identify solutions, actions or implications following on from the list of issues, problems or ideas.

Affinity diagramming is organized in four steps:

❑ Everyone lists ideas individually.

❑ They write down these ideas legibly, one per Post-it.

❑ They stick their Post-its on the board or wall (until this point the exercise is individual).

❑ As a group, discuss how to cluster ideas, and organize the clusters.

Use

❑ To organize thoughts about complex situations.

❑ To map alternative routes in an area requiring improvement.

❑ To identify the steps of a project.

Advantages

❑ Breaks down a big complex question into simpler, smaller questions.

❑ Gets participants to think individually and quickly come up with a lot of ideas without getting caught up in endless debate.

❑ Useful analytical tool that participants can apply in the workplace.

Disadvantages

❑ Time-consuming: should be reserved for high priority topics only.

❑ Requires familiarity with the subject.

Group size

❑ Small: 4–7 people (or sub-groups of the same size).

Time

❑ 30–60 minutes.

Logistics

❑ Post-its or pieces of paper and sticky tape, a wall or a big board.

Preparation

❑ Explain process clearly: stress that this tool is not a problem-solving process, but only a way to map out a problem collectively.

Mind mapping

Mind mapping is a more complex variation of brainstorming, which aims to identify all the possible components of a complex issue. This discussion is only a very succinct introduction to the technique.

In mind mapping you explore a project, an opportunity or a subject following the rules of brainstorming (free association and creative thinking). Starting in the middle of a flip chart sheet, write the word or the phrase that accurately describes the topic of the mind map. Without concern for logic or relationship, using single words, the participants write all sorts of topics or words connected to the main subject in a loose constellation around it.

The next step is to draw in the connection between these words, using colour coding to denote different types of relationships. Once the process is finished, participants will redraw the map in a clean fashion to distinguish categories and improve the visual connection between all the elements. Figure 15 shows how this training course might have been mapped using this technique. Mind maps are usually much more complex than this example.

Mind mapping follows four steps:

❑ Brainstorming ideas onto paper.

❑ Establishing connections between the ideas.

❑ Organizing elements on the mind map.

❑ Discussion and dialogue.

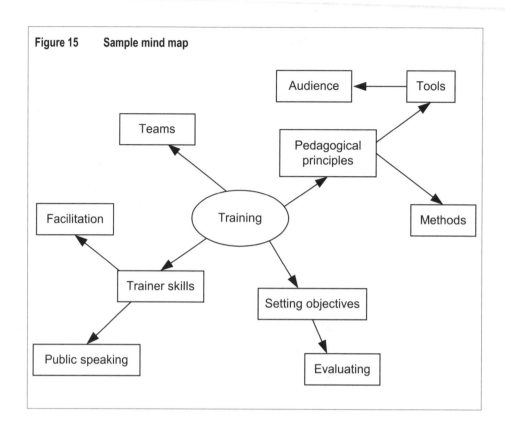

Figure 15   Sample mind map

Use

❑ To think through and visualize all elements of a complex problem.

❑ To help groups organize their thoughts around a complex issue.

❑ To memorize elements of a problem.

Advantages

❑ Frees people to think creatively.

❑ People who learn visually can retain a lot of information with the help of a mind map.

❑ Allows an exhaustive discussion.

❑ The unusual format is very stimulating.

Disadvantages

❑ Without a clear formulation of the core subject/topic the exercise can end up going in all directions.

❑ Can be intimidating for individuals whose approach is very logical and structured.

❑ It can be tedious to rewrite the mind map several times.

Group size

❑ Small, 4–7 people.

Time

❑ 30–60 minutes.

Logistics

❑ Several flip-charts or large pieces of paper tacked to the wall, colour markers or pencils.

Preparation

❑ Encourage an open, non-judgmental, tolerant atmosphere.

❑ Introduce and practise the concepts of brainstorming first.

❑ Demonstrate a simple mind map with good examples of the type of phrase and words that can be used.

❑ Explain the process.

Case study

The case study is a description of an actual, real-life situation, which the learners can use to apply the knowledge or techniques of analysis that they have learned in the course.

Case studies can vary in length and complexity. They may take just 30 minutes to read, or require several hours of study. The case study description can be as short as one page, or as long as ten, and can be accompanied with annexes such as charts, data, pictures, or even films or audio tapes.

The purpose of a case study is to put the participants in a problem-solving situation that is as close as possible to one they might face in reality. The problem, the cast of characters, the context and/or the data must be well researched and realistic so that participants get deeply involved in the activity.

A case study engages the learner in three types of activities:

❑ Analyse the situation.

❑ Make decisions.

❑ Design an action plan to implement.

Use

❑ To test understanding of key skills and concepts.

❑ To consolidate knowledge through practice.

❑ To provide concrete examples of where a theory or technique they have learned can be applied.

Advantages

❑ Breaks from the presentation mode.

❑ Illustrate a point without delivering a lecture.

❑ Can be focused on specific learning objectives.

❑ Engages participants in small-group discussions.

❑ Develops problem-solving skills.

❑ The closer the situation is to the work context of the participants, the more value-adding it will be for them.

❑ You may use several quick mini-cases to illustrate several situations.

Disadvantages

❑ Extensive preparation.

❑ If the scenario is not realistic, the case will seem artificial and will not be engaging.

❑ Without close supervision, participants may waste time exploring dead-end solutions.

❑ Time-consuming.

Group size

❑ Any (can be group-based or individual; reporting back can be oral or written).

Time

❑ Can vary depending on complexity of the case.

Logistics

❑ Extra rooms may be needed for group work.

How to write a case study

Your aim is to exercise participants' analytical and problem-solving skills. To do so, the scenario has to correspond to the targeted learning objectives. You can base it on an actual situation, changing the data, names and location in such a way that the company or individuals cannot be identified. Avoid anything that can be construed as drawn from the work context of the participants: it would be unethical to engage them in a discussion where they end up judging or evaluating decisions taken by colleagues or superiors.

A case study is composed of:

❑ A scenario.

❑ Annexes providing any information necessary to resolving the case study: data, figures or charts, descriptions of characters, locations or other important elements.

❑ A set of questions to guide the thought process.

❑ In some cases, there may be a 'right answer' that the participants are expected to find. A handout will be required to provide the correct solution to the case.

❑ A guideline for the trainer to debrief the case study (in the form of notes for the trainer).

The scenario

❑ Describe the situation to be analysed.

❑ Provide as many details as needed to make the case realistic. Too much extra information may mislead analysis; add extraneous details only if the aim is to practice distinguishing essential from non-essential information.

❑ The length of the document can range from 1 to 20 pages including annexes. Some very large case studies can require a full day of work. However, we would recommend a limited use of these.

❑ Research the scenario well, and test it before using it in training.

The questions

You should have two or more questions. The first question should address the analysis of the situation. The others can be closed or open questions, depending to your objectives.

You may ask participants to produce a document, a presentation, or present their solution in plenary. Your questions can be distributed with the case or after the participants have completed their analysis of the situation.

How to run a case study

The case study can be used to introduce the subject of a lecture that will follow, or can be used as a practical exercise to illustrate a presentation you have made. Several mini-cases could be used consecutively to illustrate several points.

When you hand out the case description, allow time for clarification questions. You may do so in plenary or by circulating between the groups.

The case study is a good method to use when you want to engage participants in group discussions. Unless you wish to test their skills and understanding individually, form sub-groups of three to five participants to discuss the case. Finding an answer to the question often requires groups to reach consensus: the friction between opinions and analysis will be rich in learning. So be sure to allow enough time for discussion.

You may decide to provide a fixed time for the completion of the case study exercise, or you may structure the discussion by providing timing guidelines for the exercise (10 minutes for analysis, 10 minutes to discuss each question, and so on).

The active part of the case study is the discussion, which takes place within groups. Listen to the conversations; take notes of interesting comments you overhear so that, if necessary, you can use them when you debrief.

Ask participants to present their analysis and solutions in the front of the group, allowing equal time to each. This creates energy and gives a more formal character to their exercise. Encourage them to use visuals such as flip charts or transparencies. You may ask them to clarify their position, but do not debrief until all the sub-groups have presented their solutions.

The debriefing is the key moment of the exercise. This is where your skills as a facilitator will be required. Your role will be to capture on the learning moment. Avoid putting people in a situation of failure. Try to steer the group back to the facts, rather than their interpretation: what are the facts, what is the problem? Encourage them to identify the core causes behind symptomatic problems. Instead of pointing to a right or wrong answer, encourage them to look at the various solutions found (for instance by posting them around the room). Then organize a discussion with the entire group to confront differences of opinions.

Just like in real life, case studies confront participants with situations that can be interpreted in a variety of ways, and lead to different decisions and different consequences. If the case is a real one and you know how it was resolved, you may provide a description of the solution, and ask the participants to discuss its pros and cons in light of their own analysis of the case.

The use of cases can be very interactive and dynamic. Sometimes participants get into heated discussions, if not near fights. Do not intervene too much; let the energy loose. To control the noise level you may wish to have the group break up into different rooms.

You may formally conclude your case study session with a small lecture, which sums up the findings and provides cognitive inputs or models.

Role-play

The role-play requires participants to act out a character in a given situation. The context and cast of characters can be provided in writing or by viewing a video sequence. After a short preparation, two or three participants act their 'role' in front of the group. Learning takes place through both observation and participation.

The exercise is dynamic, highly participative and can provide wonderful substance for debriefing.

Role-play is an excellent tool to get participants to think about attitudes, behaviours, and verbal and non-verbal communication. It can be a way of practising communication styles in management, sales, leadership, customer services and so on. In contrast to lectures and presentations, it confronts learners with real situations. Skills, attitudes and behaviours can be practised, and feedback from the audience (rather than just from the trainer) is a great way to reinforce and improve the target skills or attitudes.

There are many variations on role-play, of which these are a few:

❑ Simulation of an encounter (interview, sales pitch, etc.).

❑ Role reversal: participants assume the role of others with whom they normally interact on the job.

❑ Role rotation: a first round of the role-play is enacted and then pairs shift roles.

Use

❑ To practise new behaviours or new techniques.

❑ To give participants a sense of what a situation may feel like.

❑ To develop skills to handle specific situations (interviews, sales, mediation).

❑ To raise awareness of a communication issue.

Advantages

❑ Participative, engaging and challenging.

❑ Because role-plays are 'off the job', participants may be more objective, more relaxed.

❑ Participants gain quick insights on themselves and others.

❑ Participants learn how to use each other as resources.

Disadvantages

❑ Some people may be anxious and suffer a form of stage fright.

❑ Needs to be timed very well so that it does not drag on too long.

❑ Depends on a climate of trust where jokes or cynical and critical comments are avoided. Limit the judgement; build on the learning.

Group size

❑ Small to medium.

Time

❑ One hour.

Logistics

❑ Video equipment if you plan to introduce the role-play on video.

How to write a role-play

The role-play scenario should be very short (at most 10 lines). It is a simple snapshot of a situation: an encounter, a telephone exchange, an interview. You need to provide the essential information about the situation in which the parties are meeting or communicating. If necessary you may have a line or two on the character each player is acting. Keep it simple and make sure that everyone understands what he or she is meeting or communicating about.

You may add some complexity to a basic scenario by slightly varying the information provided to each group or player, if this is realistic.

How to run a role-play

It is not always easy to enter into role-playing. The 'players' need to be given enough time to understand the situation, role and character.

Because role-play can be quite threatening or challenging for some people, you need to establish some basic principles. In your briefing, stress that the objective is not to judge the performances but to learn, and that there is no right or wrong way to act the situation out. Review the basic rules of feedback and warn the audience that negative comments can be hurtful. Your role as a trainer is to create a positive learning atmosphere.

When you have handed out the text and scenarios, allow time for clarification, and time for preparation in private.

Set the classroom up so that everyone can see the players. It is often easiest to move tables aside and set chairs around the 'stage area'.

Each acting sequence may last 5 to 15 minutes. More than 15 minutes is counterproductive because it gets boring. You may interrupt the play at any point, either to capitalize on a learning moment or because the characters are off mark. When interrupting the players, you may involve the audience and ask questions like: 'What do you see going on here? Do you agree with what is going on?'

The debriefing stage has to be dynamic and involve both the audience and the players. Simple questions like: 'How are you feeling right now? What did you experience, what problems did you encounter?' will encourage the players to analyse their choices and help release any tension they may have been feeling.

Some tips on running role-plays

❑ Thank the players and encourage the group to applaud the performance.

❑ Be empathic with the players and moderate the criticism of the audience.

❑ Balance critical feedback with positive comments; stress areas to improve rather than negative points.

❑ Restate the opinions of the audience.

❑ Acknowledge the fact that the first pair or trio to start the role-play is in a disadvantaged position.

❑ Judge behaviour, not people.

❑ The more you can connect the performances to what is taking place back at work, the more relevant the debriefing will be. Questions like 'Does this remind you of anything? Have you seen this type of situation before? Where?' will help connect the role-play with real-life situations.

❑ If tension is running high or if participants seem uncomfortable, use humour and empathy to defuse the situation.

❏ If someone does not wish to act, they should feel free not to; they will participate anyway through observation and feedback.

❏ Don't worry if everyone does not get a chance to act because you run out of time: they will have learned a lot by preparing, observing and participating in the debriefing.

Simulations

The objective of a simulation is to rehearse skills or behaviours required in a specific professional setting. In contrast, the role-play asks the 'actors' to apply their own judgement and their own choices in a more spontaneous way to a given situation, and focuses learning on perception and feelings. In simulations, the participants are expected to apply a very specific set of skills, and are assessed on how well they succeed. Feedback on a simulation will point out what the player did well, what they need to improve, whether they reached the objectives they had set themselves, and so on. In the role-play the learning takes place while observing and acting. In the simulation the learning takes place while acting. The result of the simulation is the indicator of how each party did: did he or she succeed, and if not, why?

There are many types of simulations, from simple ones to more complex cases, which can last a full day. You can have simulations of sales contract negotiations, negotiations with trade unions or employees' representatives, meetings, performance evaluation sessions, and so on.

In its format, the simulation is a combination of case study and role-play. The scenario describes the general situation. In addition, each participant receives a set of instructions and information relevant to the part they will play. The simulation involves an analysis of the situation, the development of a strategy and the crafting of an action plan by each party. These then guide their positions and choices during the course of the simulation. The scenario, as in the case study, can have several annexes providing data, figures, and description of characters.

Complex simulations should come at the end of a course because they require participants to integrate the various parts of their learning into a whole. As in the role-play, the debriefing will be the key learning moment. You may wish to use video recordings or one observer to enrich the discussion and to feed back reactions to the participants.

Use

❏ To integrate the many parts of learning into a whole.

❏ To practise what was learned in a situation close to one found on the job.

❏ To evaluate how well skills or behaviour have been integrated.

Advantages

❏ Close to real life: creates a more competitive atmosphere between the parties involved, and can therefore foster emulation among participants.

❏ Engaging: participants will remember the case they played in for a very long time.

Disadvantages

❏ Very time-consuming to prepare and run.

❏ Very dependent on the quality of the scenario and the debriefing.

❑ Can cause conflict and tension among participants in the simulation.

❑ Some people may be much more participative than others; if people hang back it can jeopardize the success of the simulation for others.

Group size

❑ Because of the time involved, this approach is best suited to medium-sized groups. Sub-groups or teams should be constituted with 3–4 people.

Time

❑ A simulation exercise can be limited to 30–60 minutes. But more complex simulations, as noted, can be extended over much longer periods.

Logistics

❑ You need a dedicated room; video recording equipment can help with assessment.

How to write a simulation

Simulation writing requires extensive research and excellent writing skills. As for role-plays, the scenario chosen may be an actual situation, modifying key details. You may need to conduct interviews and gather data for the case.

The description of the simulation context, and the position and interests of each party involved in the exercise must be very precise.

How to run a simulation

Many of the principles of running role-plays and case studies apply also to simulations:

❑ Let each participant read the simulation and understand the situation.

❑ Allow participants time to analyse the case and develop their strategy.

❑ Agree on a meeting time when the simulation will take place.

❑ Prepare the room so that everything is ready for the enactment: tables, chairs, paper, etc. If you wish to record the simulation on video, install the equipment and make sure the camera is well placed.

❑ Debrief extensively. Review how each party did. What was the result? At first let the discussion flow freely. Participants need to express their satisfaction, their discontent and their frustration. Once they have expressed themselves, you may start structuring the debriefing according to a set of pre-established guidelines.

Experiential learning exercises

Experiential learning exercises are simulations that serve as metaphors for a situation, a problem or a group dynamic the trainer wants to illustrate. A problem with very remote resemblance to reality is given to the group to resolve. The group accomplishes the task and then the activity is debriefed.

Because the exercise has little resemblance to any real situation, the participants tend to be quite authentic in their behaviour and they 'catch themselves in the act of being themselves', with their natural resistances or difficulties in communicating or in working effectively together.

Here is an example of such an exercise. You hand a rope to the group. The task is for the team, to create, blindfolded and without speaking, a perfect square in two minutes. For this you give them 15 minutes preparation time, during which they plan and rehearse how they are going to do the task. When the 15 minutes are up ask participants to put the blindfolds on. After two minutes tell them to remove the blindfolds, and start the debriefing. Did they achieve the goal? How did they do it? How effective were they in their planning? Did everyone understand his or her role? Numerous themes can be explored in this way, from teamwork to planning, problem solving and communication. The key stage of course is the debriefing, where the trainer will guide the group in reflecting on the experience, and relating it to the learning objectives.

Use

❑ To illustrate behaviours and group dynamics in a fun way.

❑ To encourage reflection about these issues.

Advantages

❑ Highly versatile exercises that can be used for team building, communication, leadership, management, problem solving, decision making, change management and much more.

❑ Address behaviours and attitudes, which can seldom be effectively dealt with in a lecture.

❑ Create a surprise effect and suggest individual reflection.

❑ Team-building; help create ties between participants.

❑ Engaging and fun; encourage people to let down their guard. Participants will be more talkative and honest with each other.

❑ Because they seem to have little to do with work, they encourage people to be themselves.

❑ The metaphor can be a striking one that participants will remember.

❑ Create a common frame of reference.

Disadvantages

❑ Not applicable everywhere: in some cultures, participants may be reluctant to touch each other, or they may find 'playing games' demeaning.

❑ If the activity is not presented in the context of the learning objectives, it may be experienced as just a game or energizer rather than an opportunity for learning.

❑ If the metaphor is unclear, participants will not make the link with any real situation.

Group size

❑ The maximum size is probably around 15 people. Beyond this number certain group members will be passive.

Time

❑ Variable: an entire session including debriefing can last as much as an hour. Place importance on the latter phase, since this is where much of the learning takes place.

Logistics

❑ Experiential learning can take place inside the classroom or outdoors. There is an advantage in going outdoors if you need more space to move around, but make sure that your group will not draw a crowd of curious onlookers!

Preparation

If you are not familiar with the chosen exercise you need to either watch it with a group or participate in it beforehand. Once you understand the dynamics of the exercise you can modify the rules or apply it for other purposes.

Some tips

❑ Make sure the metaphor is clear so that the participants will make a connection to a real situation.

❑ Explain why you are doing the exercise, what objective is being met.

❑ Do not refer to the activity as a 'game' but as an 'exercise'.

❑ If you are using several activities, make sure they increase in complexity. Start with an easy task.

❑ Some adults feel that these are games for children and might act cynical or be reluctant to participate. Select exercises that appeal to their intelligence.

❑ Be aware of cultural differences that might influence participants' willingness to engage in experiential activities.

❑ Spend ample time in debriefing. Make sure participants go beyond talking about the activity and actually discuss its meaning to them in the workplace.

Clinic

The clinic is a one-on-one session between the trainer and one participant, or between two participants, with the aim of giving feedback and coaching in a specific area. The clinic is usually used after self-assessments or personality profiles, or even with psychometric testing. It is a format where participants get to learn more about themselves with the assistance of either the trainer or a colleague. An essential condition is that participation should be voluntary. As a matter of course, confidentiality of the results must be strictly respected.

Use

❑ To provide feedback, coaching.
❑ To carry out reviews, appraisals, 360-degree feedback.

Advantages

❑ Helps people grow and develop.
❑ Opportunity for self-reflection.

Disadvantages

❑ Participants need to have the right mindset and be open to criticism. If not, feedback may put people on the defensive and make them feel hurt and attacked.

❑ If colleagues or group participants are conducting the clinic with each other, the rules need to be well defined to avoid defensive, hurt or critical reactions.

Group size

❑ Two people.

Time

❑ As needed.

Logistics

❑ Access to a private room.

Preparation

The clinic is a one-on-one feedback or coaching session. If you are organizing a clinic to go over the results of a tool, such as a simulation or a 360-degree assessment, it is assumed that the participants have received an explanation of the tool, and the research and theory that supports it. This background information is essential to validate the instrument in the eyes of the participants and to provide a framework for understanding it.

During the clinic, be aware that your words carry significant weight for the participants; think carefully about what you will say and make sure your comments are constructive. Criticisms should be presented as opportunities for growth. You should be able to support all your comments with facts and observations.

Start each clinic session by setting a clear time for the session and emphasizing the confidential nature of the exchange. Reassure the participant that you, the trainer, will keep the information confidential and will not divulge it to his or her boss or human resources department. Acquire some basic information on the person you are providing the clinic to – profession, personal data and background. The clinic should be a give and take: ask the participant if he or she agrees with your comments, and leave time at the end for questions. A fundamental assumption is that the information you are basing your opinion on is somewhat biased; therefore, it should always be validated by the participant.

Psychometric instruments

Psychometric instruments are tools that measure some aspect of personality or individual ability. There are a lot of these instruments available on the market, from personality profiles to specific skills assessment (communication, leadership, decision making, problem solving, adaptability to change or management styles). Some companies that produce these tests require that you be accredited to administer them. However quite a few are available to purchase, or can be downloaded for free on the Internet.

As you know, people love to learn about themselves and to receive feedback. Psychometric tests can be used in plenary if they are self-scoring, or on a one-on-one basis if they require individual feedback. They can be briefed and debriefed from the front of the room and you can have people pair up to deepen their understanding of their results.

You should always emphasize the relative validity of those tests; they are only as accurate as the information that is put into them. Their scientific value is relative. Furthermore, you should deal cautiously with the information you gather: it must remain confidential, and in no circumstances should you be required to share it with a participant's employer.

Use

❑ To deepen participants' self-awareness of specific behaviours, attitudes or skills.

❑ To illustrate issues of behaviour, attitudes, and soft skills.

Advantages

- ❑ Intriguing and stimulating.
- ❑ Look serious and professional.
- ❑ Stimulate discussion.
- ❑ Provide a break from traditional teaching formats (lecture) and encourage further investigation.

Disadvantages

- ❑ All but the simplest self-scoring tests require extensive analysis, either by hand or with a computer.
- ❑ Tests are not available in all languages; if you use a language that is not the participants' mother tongue, they will take a long time to fill in the test.
- ❑ Can be long and tedious to complete.
- ❑ Participants often question the validity of the responses they get.

Group size

- ❑ Any.

Time

- ❑ Variable.

Logistics

- ❑ No equipment required.

Preparation

Make sure you understand the research and the background theory of the instrument you use. You will face numerous questions from participants so it is crucial you understand the test and are able to provide concrete, realistic examples. Your inability to do so will very quickly cause the participants to become sceptical about the test.

Self-scoring or questionnaire-type instruments may be filled out ahead of time, for instance the evening before the course session. In class, you can guide the participants through the scoring of the test. You may also introduce the theory underlying the test after they have filled it out but before they score it. In this way participants assess themselves while scoring, and then validate what the test tells them.

When instruments are not self-scoring, you will have to total the scores yourself or send them for evaluation to the company that sells the tools. This can take time.

Plan the session carefully in order to keep the audience awake and engaged. Encourage participants to share their results and learn from each other.

Field trips

Sometimes it is useful to step out of the classroom and take your group of trainees to visit exhibitions, companies, producers, suppliers, and governmental or non-governmental institutions. The objective of a field trip is more than just learning: it is an opportunity to meet people, speak with specialists and bond with members of the group. Field trips can be quite memorable experiences; sometimes the trip itself can be a great bonding experience regardless of the destination.

Field trips require extensive preparation. You need to know the place you are visiting, establish contacts with the people you will meet, and organize guided visits, meetings, interviews or presentations as necessary. Although field trips can be organized in a cost-effective fashion, they often entail additional expenses, such as travel, which are not always on the budget.

Use

❑ To add a practical, realistic dimension to the course.

❑ To build team spirit in the group in a non-classroom environment.

Advantages

❑ Participants gain new perspectives.

❑ Field trips are stimulating and energizing.

❑ Help build networks.

❑ Good break from traditional teaching.

Disadvantages

❑ Time-consuming.

❑ Need to be well planned; if there are going to be interviews and presentations you need to assess the quality of these.

❑ Can be expensive and require logistical planning.

Group size

❑ Any (but the larger the group the more complex the logistics).

Time

❑ Several hours to several days.

Logistics

❑ Transport and meals; accommodation for overnight trips. A list of what to bring or how to dress for the planned activity (for instance, comfortable shoes for walking, bathing suit, informal or formal clothes, note-pad, etc.) is very helpful. Remember to bring a camera or appoint a volunteer to take pictures of the trip – these will be much appreciated.

Preparation

Prepare field trips thoroughly. To avoid unnecessary waits and frustrations, make sure the logistics are well organized and run smoothly (transport, meals, appointments, etc.). If you are going to an exhibition, visit it ahead of time so that you can talk about it to the group before the trip. If you plan to visit production sites, make sure you have a guide. Meet or call the speakers, guides or presenters beforehand. The more you prepare, the better you will be able to prepare participants, and the more they will learn from the trip.

Module 5

Delivering training programmes

Getting started

The first step to starting a course session, seminar or workshop is to create the right conditions for learning. Your job as a trainer is to foster an environment in which people are relaxed, open and interested. Only then can they begin to really listen, participate and learn.

As you walk towards the front of the class on the first day, you should be aware of what is going through the minds of your audience:

❑ In most cases they don't know who you are or what your qualifications are.

❑ They are probably feeling insecure, and wondering what is going to happen, what will be expected of them. These feelings of insecurity, of which they may not even be conscious, can prevent them from fully participating in the course.

❑ Often the participants do not know each other, and are wondering who everyone else is and what are they doing here.

❑ People tend to be cautious in a new situation and this natural cautiousness tends to make them quiet and reserved.

You should therefore anticipate your audience's questions and insecurities and address them before they have a chance to be voiced.

Getting acquainted

Point 1: Who you are

Introduce yourself briefly in five sentences or less. More may seem like bragging, which your audience will see through right away. You want people to have a positive view of you. Trying to fool them rarely works.

Point 2: Questions

Anticipate the questions or concerns people may have. This allows you to quickly address them.

Using presentation software or a flip chart, you can provide a broad overview of the agenda, that is, what will happen, where and when.

Be sure to cover logistics: for example, restrooms, coffee break areas, transportation, and so on. Try to think of whatever may be a concern.

Point 3: Who is participating

We are social animals. We want to know who is around us so that we know how to function in this new social group that has been formed for the purpose of training. We want to identify similarities and differences and find out who we might like to get to know better, who we might want to avoid, and so on.

Depending on the size of the group, there are several ways to get people comfortable with each other.

The simplest and most common approach is to have participants introduce themselves one at a time. It is best to give them an indication of the type of information to give, for example: name, company, function and position and why he or she is attending the course.

This approach works only for small groups. Beyond 15 people, individual self-presentation takes too long, becomes boring and can be intimidating. Moreover, no one will be able to remember anything much.

A second approach for small groups up to 20 people is called 'paired introductions'. People pair up with someone they do not know and conduct a brief interview around a set of questions you provide, for example: your name, the company you work for, your role in the company, how long have you worked there and your favourite pastime (for a more personal note). Then each person introduces their partner to the group as a whole. This creates a bit more intimacy within the group, because initially people are speaking one on one, exchanging more personal information, and then connecting back to the group.

For groups beyond 20 there is no manageable way to introduce everyone. But there are other techniques that help members of the group become acquainted with each other and identify similarities and differences. These approaches capitalize on the need to identify with others.

You could, for instance ask participants to identify themselves by their sector of industry, instructing people from, say, the electronics industry to stand on one side of the room, and those who work in the chemical industry to move to the other side of the room. If they are to remain seated, ask them to raise their hand. In an actual situation, you would ask a series of questions so that the entire group would divide several times according to different criteria. This also gives you the opportunity to ask questions about the groupings you have formed.

Point 4: Cautiousness

At the beginning of a programme do not expect a high level of participation. Put the audience at ease by showing you know who they are, what they do, and what they can contribute.

Opening exercises

There are many ways of starting off a course – a couple have already been introduced above. Some trainers like to start with opening exercises. These help accomplish the following goals:

❑ **Group building:** as mentioned earlier, some exercises can help participants to become acquainted with each other and create a spirit of cooperation and interdependence.

❑ **On the spot assessment:** some exercises will give you an idea of the attitudes, knowledge and experience of the participants.

❑ **Immediate learning involvement:** some exercises help create initial interest in the training topic.

Group building

The objective is to help participants become acquainted with each other and lay the basis for future teamwork. Several forms of introduction were discussed above. Here is a more involved and playful exercise that you could try in the first session.

Two truths and a lie (15 participants maximum)

This is a quick way to let participants discover more about each other, in a fun and playful way. Ask each participant to think about two true facts about themselves and make up one false one. Those facts should be new to the group. Each participant takes turn telling these facts to the group. Everyone votes to decide which of the three facts are true and which is a lie. Tally those up on a flip chart. Once everyone has told three facts, ask them to identify the lie. The person who persuaded most people that his or her lie was a truth is the winner.

On-the-spot assessment

There are several forms of on-the-spot assessment (these are discussed in module 6). The easiest is just to ask the audience for input verbally. However, you may also ask participants to form small groups and discuss one of these topics:

❑ Share their learning goals or expectations;

❑ Raise questions or concerns they may have about the course;

❑ Relate their knowledge and experience to the course topics;

❑ List successes and problems they have experienced that are relevant to the course;

❑ Explore their opinions and attitudes about the course.

Let us imagine that you ask the audience to share their learning goals and expectations. Write them on a flip chart. Once everyone has expressed his or her goals, you can launch into a description of what the course will (and will not) bring them. This allows you to readjust expectations.

Immediate learning involvement

It is possible to design an exercise as part of your course introduction.

One method is to prepare 8 to 10 assertions related to the subject of your course. They should be thought provoking and invite disagreement: for example, 'the most difficult task of management is keeping up with technology', or 'as long as workers get appropriate pay, they will be content with their work'. Write the statements up on the board or flip chart.

Distribute three cards to everyone: a green one (I agree), a yellow one (I have no opinion) and a red one (I disagree).

Read each statement slowly and ask the members of the group to vote with their cards. Record the group's votes next to each statement. After all the statements have been voted upon, start the debate on the statement where there is most disagreement.

The purpose of an opening exercise of this kind is to demonstrate the complexity of a topic, show the diversity of opinion that exists in the group and start everyone thinking about the subject.

There are many types of such activities; you may invent some of your own. Their benefit is that they get participants thinking and learning from the very first minute in the classroom.

Encouraging participation

The aim of every trainer is to create involvement and active participation. This may not always be easy, as it depends on the type of audience, as well as their cultural background. Here are 10 tips to encourage participation, which may be used at any point in the course of a training programme.

- ❑ **Small-group discussions.** This classic tool has participants break into small groups of three to five people in order to share, discuss, and record information. Use this method when you have sufficient time to process questions and to hear groups report back.

- ❑ **Pairing up.** Without reorganizing your audience, ask participants to work on a task or have a quick discussion with the person sitting next to them. This technique is good when you do not have time for small group discussions, but still want people to discuss and express their opinions.

- ❑ **Progressive conversations.** Ask participants to pair up, discuss and agree on certain points. After a while, ask two pairs to combine and share what they discussed. You may do a third round to reach a group size of eight, who will present the final result of their discussion. This technique allows you to discuss a wide range of ideas very quickly. It tends to bring results faster than group discussions where the same group talk about a single topic for a certain length of time.

- ❑ **Probing.** Go around the group and obtain short responses to key questions. You may move about in the room and place yourself in front of the person to ask a question, or call on them by name. Use probing when you want to obtain something quickly from each participant: definitions, figures, opinions and so on. Do not intimidate your audience, and allow them to pass their turn if they wish.

- ❑ **Panels.** Invite a small number of participants to present their views to the entire group.

- ❑ **Quizzes.** Check knowledge on a given subject by asking four or five short questions.

- ❑ **Fishbowl.** Ask some members of the group to form a discussion circle and have the remaining participants form a listening circle around them. Every few minutes bring new people into the inner circle to continue the discussion and send the same number out. Use the fishbowl to bring focus to large group discussions. Although time-consuming, this is the best method for combining large- and small-group discussions.

- ❑ **Open sharing.** Ask a question and open it up to the entire group without structuring the discussion. Use this technique when you are certain that several members want to participate. If you are worried that too many people will speak, say that you will take only four or five contributions.

- ❑ **Anonymous cards.** Pass out index cards and request anonymous answers to your questions. Have the completed cards passed around the group. Discuss the responses with the group.

- ❑ **Questionnaires.** Design a short questionnaire to be filled out and tallied on the spot. Use questionnaires to obtain data quickly and in a quantifiable form. Tally the questionnaire on the spot and discuss the result with the group.

Many of these options allow you to sit back and let the participants take charge. However sometimes the group needs your leadership. Your role is to facilitate the flow of comments and to synthesize their thinking. It is not always necessary to interject after each comment or answer. However, there are some tricks for supporting and encouraging people to express themselves:

- ❑ **Paraphrase** what someone said so that the participant knows he or she has been heard, and so that the others can hear a concise summary of what has just been said.

- ❑ **Check** your understanding of what was said or ask a participant to clarify what was said.

- ❑ **Congratulate** your trainees on an interesting or insightful comment. Be careful not to always congratulate the same ones.

- ❑ **Expand** on what the trainees said, quote supporting data or theory, or express your view on what was said.

- ❑ **Energize** the discussion by quickening the pace, using humour or probing the group for more contributions. Tease, joke, encourage – do what is needed to gently pry them out of their silence.

- ❑ **Disagree** gently with something that was said in order to stimulate further discussion. Avoid putting people on the spot if you want them to participate. Tell them that it is all right to be wrong and that everyone is here to learn.

- ❑ **Mediate** between two or three participants with diverging opinions. Mention that part of the learning process is to disagree, and remind them to do so in a positive way.

- ❑ **Synthesize** ideas and opinions. Show the complementarities between different opinions that have been expressed.

- ❑ **Change the process** by altering the method of participation or by prompting the group to evaluate issues that have been raised during the discussion. If you are leading a discussion with a large audience, break it into small groups to explore one aspect more thoroughly.

- ❑ **Record** what is said on a flip chart to show the interaction and links between all the views expressed. Highlight the richness of the group's expertise.

If you apply these tricks you will find yourself facilitating rather than leading. By doing so, you will empower the group to take charge of the learning process, which should be one of your ultimate objectives.

Developing a lecture or presentation

Lectures and presentations are both affirmative (or presentational) teaching methods, although there are several ways to you can deliver a lecture, some of which follow an interrogative rather than a presentational method. The fundamental assumption of the lecture is that the lecturer has knowledge that he or she transmits to the learner through an uninterrupted speech. Because of this, promoters of active and discovery training often criticize presentational methods for being too passive. However, it is the method most prevalent in formal learning, and therefore the most familiar to most participants. Furthermore, lecturing is a time-effective way of communicating information and theory. Short 10–15 minute lectures, or lecturettes, are a good way of starting off or concluding a topic and can be combined with more active methods.

Unfortunately, presentation methods are often chosen for the wrong reasons:

❑ The trainer might choose to lecture because he or she lacks the capacity to adapt the content to the level of his/her audience.

❑ A poor teacher will always rely on this method, rather than engage the group in active thinking, which is relatively more difficult to organize and mediate.

❑ Egocentric presenters choose the lecture because it flatters their high opinion of themselves.

❑ The inexperienced trainer will abuse this method, as it is the easiest and most obvious (because it is so familiar).

If chosen for the right reasons, however the lecture can be very effective. In this section we will provide some general guidelines on structuring, preparing and delivering lectures that engage the audience.

Types of presentations

A lecture is the oral presentation of a sum of ideas and concepts that form a coherent whole. There are other types of oral presentations. Here are a few examples, but you may easily find more:

❑ A salesperson makes a presentation on his or her products;

❑ A lawyer makes a pleading at the bench;

❑ A trainer explains a process or outlines an argument.

Although these three types of speech are all oral presentations, the last one is the only one that contains a pedagogical element. It is part of a coherent pedagogical process, which aims at stimulating and promoting the acquisition of knowledge, know-how, skills and behaviours. The types of presentational methods that a trainer can call upon are described below.

The lecture

The lecture is a speech with a structured content or argument, much like an essay. In general the outline of the lecture is defined ahead of time and the presenter does not digress from the original intent. The trainer usually does not expect any give-and-take with the participants during the lecture. However, a question time should be provided for at the end of the lecture.

The demonstrative lecture

This form of lecture provides instruction through demonstration (how to fill out questionnaires, how to keep accounting records, how to use software, etc.). It is used when introducing a new process or technique. The lecture plan is strictly chronological, working systematically through the steps of the process. In the demonstrative lecture, the trainer does not expect any input from the participants, other than requests for clarification.

The interrogative presentation

The trainer prepares a presentation as well as a series of questions to stimulate the discussion and the thinking of the participants. The questions must be fairly closed, and answerable by a correct answer ('is it A or B?' rather than 'what do you think about A and B?'). Only after the group has found the right answers does the trainer continue the presentation, or follow on with a new question. This presentation method requires participants to practise inductive reasoning, and calls for considerable trainer–trainee interaction.

The active presentation

A short lecture can also be improvised whenever a learning moment arises. Here a key principle applies: the presentation must never precede the experimentation phase; it must either accompany it, or follow it. The trainer encourages questions, interaction and contributions rather than lecturing in an uninterrupted fashion.

The lecturette

A short 10–15 minute lecture, it helps to frame a subject. It is a favoured tool to introduce concepts, theory and methodology, or to communicate data and information in a synthetic way.

Planning and delivering presentations

A presentation must be structured logically, and carefully planned before being filled out with arguments, illustrations and so on. Preparing a lecture requires you to pay attention to the following elements:

Preparation

❑ Define clearly the key messages you want to communicate. Lay them out as bullet points. Allocate a time for each section of the presentation.

❑ Rehearse your presentation out loud – when reading silently we tend to read faster. You need to know exactly how long your presentation will last. You can then cut the content of the lecture to fit the allotted time span. Always allow for extra time: delivery in front of the classroom tends to be slower than when you practise because of anxiety and interruptions. Since the trainer is the only one to speak, time management of a lecture-based lesson plan is easier than with interactive methods.

❑ Prepare the visual and support material that will accompany the presentation.

Length

❑ The length of the presentation must be calculated to keep the audience engaged. An optimal length is 20 minutes for a passive presentation (no questions from the audience), and 40 minutes for an active presentation (where questions are allowed). Our advice is not to exceed 40 minutes.

Timing

❑ Avoid planning a formal presentation after a meal, when people tend to be sleepy. Prefer the morning sessions.

Writing presentations

Presentations require considerable preparation. The time this takes can be cut down if you plan before you start to write. It is essential to define the objective of the presentations first, and to prepare a detailed outline of the points that will best communicate the information or arguments. You should follow the classic structure of the essay, with an introduction, a body and a conclusion.

Objectives

Start by thinking of the objectives of the presentation:

❑ What do I wish to argue, demonstrate, or illustrate in this presentation?

❑ What reaction do I want to provoke?

❑ If the audience were to retain only one or two ideas from this presentation, what would they be?

If you answer these questions honestly, you will be successful in focusing your presentation and avoiding the common pitfall of getting sidetracked into interesting but non-essential digressions.

Structure

Your presentation will be most intelligible if it conforms to the basic structure of the essay: introduction, body, and conclusion.

❑ Introduction: I say what I will say;

❑ Body: I say it;

❑ Conclusion: I say what I have just said.

This may seem like a lot of repetition to you, but to a trainee for whom the topic is new, it will not.

❑ **The introduction** presents the subject in broad terms. A striking introduction catches the audience's attention and makes them want to keep listening. The purpose of the introduction is also to link the topic of the lecture to the wider context, by explaining its connection to what came before (previous class, activity or course), and its importance to the trainees in their workplace.

❑ **The body** is the core of the presentation. Here you make your points and argue them convincingly.

❑ **The conclusion** closes the talk by recalling the key points that were made. It can also give an indication of what follows in the next section of the course.

Outline

Detailed outlining of the body of the presentation is the key to a well-structured lecture. The outline allows you to organize your points and argue them logically. You can do so in several different ways:

❑ **Thematical**: the subject is divided into different topics or themes, each of which is discussed in turn (much like this module).

❑ **Binary**: each point is discussed in terms of advantages and disadvantages.

❑ **Chronological**: historical time or the order of a process determines the order of the lecture (for instance if you are talking about the development of a technology over time, or explaining the steps of a procedure).

❑ **Questioning**: the subject is discussed according to questions – when, what, who, where, how, how much, etc.

❑ **Logical**: the logical link of each idea is emphasized. What is it? What does it do? Why use it?

Language and style

Awareness of language is key to writing engaging, striking lectures that your audience will remember (that is, after all, your final objective!). Try to always follow these few guidelines:

❑ Choose simple, everyday words, rather than technical or academic jargon whenever you can.

❑ Use a polite, conversational, not overly formal, tone.

❑ Use short sentences and common tenses.

❑ Be precise in your choice of words. Avoid catch-all words.

❑ Alternate concrete, abstract, and metaphorical illustrations.

❑ Explain any jargon, acronyms, technical words and foreign words you use.

❑ Use linking words and expressions (conjunctions) such as 'first of all', 'this is why', 'therefore', 'nevertheless', 'thus', etc. to provide a logical link between ideas.

❑ Write on the whiteboard or blackboard all names, technical words, foreign terms, acronyms, abbreviations, numbers, dates and so on.

❑ Rouse your audience and make them think by asking rhetorical questions (questions to which you do not expect an answer from the audience – you answer them yourself in your lecture).

Adapting to the group

To be effective, the lecturer must adapt the tone and level of the lecture to the audience rather than expect the audience to adapt. Try to use terms and expressions that are accessible to the group you are addressing. Profession, educational level and habits, culture: these are some factors you should take into account.

Different learning styles within the audience should also be taken into account. In module 1 we introduced Kolb's four learning styles. In addition, neuro-linguistic programming shows that we all have a preference for either visual, auditory or kinaesthetic inputs. Make sure to appeal to all these styles in your presentation: use written text, visuals, video, discussion and manipulations to get your points across.

You should make ample use of illustrations. As the saying goes, 'a picture is worth a thousand words'. An illustration produces a mental image that strikes the imagination of the participant; this eases the learning process. The listener understands abstract concepts and theories better if they are illustrated by a concrete example, or bolstered by concrete evidence. To illustrate is to provide facts (names, figures, etc.), examples, anecdotes, analogies, etc. Adapting to your audience will mean choosing illustrations that are close to their reality and experience.

Speaking from notes

If the topic is new to you, or you are anxious about presenting in front of an audience, written notes can be of great help. In fact, you should not try to lecture without notes unless you have extensive experience of public speaking. Do not, however, fall into the trap of writing a full text that you will then be tempted to read, at the risk of losing the attention of your audience. Here are a few tips on speaking notes.

❑ Take notes on index cards or on horizontal A4 paper. Write large, use colour for emphasis, and do not cram too much into one page.

❑ Outline introduction and conclusion on one page each.

❑ Outline the key ideas for each section of the presentation, the illustrations and the visual supports, if any on one page each.

❑ Write all the data you might not remember precisely (numbers, dates, names ...) and write down in full any definitions you may need to quote.

Delivery

How the trainer speaks, stands, dresses, makes eye contact with the audience will influence the success of the presentation. Our main tool for delivering a presentation, however, is the voice. A few tips on delivery can help improve your delivery.

❑ **Speed.** To give weight to your message you must speak at a medium pace, slow down and pause frequently. You alternate between a faster pace and a slower pace. The more varied the pace is, the more you keep your audience attentive.

❑ **Pitch.** Unfortunately for many women, audiences prefer lower voices, finding them reassuring. High-pitched voices tend to excite and tire. If your voice is high-pitched you will notice that when you speak louder it gets higher. You should watch out for this tendency, as you may be perceived as strident.

❑ **Volume.** The volume of the voice must be adjusted to the size of the room, and to the size of the group. You should try to project your voice without shouting, as actors do. At the beginning of the presentation, ask people at the back of the room if they can hear you – adjust your volume accordingly.

❑ **Articulation.** The slower we talk the more we articulate. Make a conscious effort to articulate well.

❑ **Intonation.** The way we use pitch in language conveys meaning (for instance in the rising tone of a question). We use intonation to stress certain key words, and convey excitement, disapproval, anger and other emotions. The more intonation you use, the more you will seem convinced of what you are saying, and the more you will convince your audience. Good intonation will make your presentation lively and engaging.

Making eye contact

As mentioned above, voice is not the only factor to consider. How the speaker is dressed, stands, moves around, and especially makes eye contact with the audience is also key.

When speaking to a large audience, we tend to look at the first row, at the risk of losing the attention of the last row. Good speakers establish contact and communication with the entire audience by looking right and left, to the front and back. Looking at the audience also allows the speaker to gauge reactions by reading facial expressions (approval, disapproval, understanding, lack of understanding, boredom). These expressions will tell the speaker whether he or she should slow down, provide more illustrations or move on rapidly to the next topic.

Here are some tips on eye contact:

❑ Look people in the eye briefly; don't stare.

❑ Some room layouts and presentation choices require you to stay in front of the room, but the more you are able to move about the group, the more contact you will have.

❑ Do not turn your back on the participants, particularly when you use overheads; consult them from the overhead projector glass, not from the screen. This allows you to keep facing your audience.

❑ Use hand gestures and facial expressions for emphasis (but too much gesticulation is distracting).

Preparing materials for a presentation

You will probably require several types of materials to support the spoken part of the presentation.

Visual materials. You may prepare outlines, charts, figures, definitions, or other visuals that you will deliver using a projector, or copy onto a flip-chart or blackboard.

Handouts. You may choose to provide the audience with written materials to take away from the presentation. These could include the full text or outline of the presentation, a copy of the slides or overheads, a topical article mentioned in the lecture or a bibliography.

Supports. Flip charts, whiteboards, blackboards, overhead projectors and slide projectors are means to deliver the visual inputs you have prepared, but also to provide information as you go along, for instance noting acronyms, figures or technical terms that crop up in your presentation. We will discuss below how you can take advantage of the possibilities of different supports.

Flip chart

Flip charts are sheets of paper hinged together at the top that can be flipped over to present information. They are like giant notepads set on an easel. They are very useful because they can be transported anywhere in a room. Several flip charts will be handy for group work.

You can copy out the outline of the presentation, draw charts, and write quotes, definitions and statements beforehand on the flip chart. When preparing flip chart sheets, or when writing on them during a presentation, follow some common-sense guidelines:

❑ Write large.

❑ Use colours effectively for emphasis and logic.

❑ Prepare main points of the outline beforehand; fill in with details and data during the presentation.

❑ Mark pages of the prepared flip chart with a number or sign that will allow you to turn directly to the right page during the course of the presentation.

❑ Make speaking notes to yourself in pencil directly on the flip chart; these will not be visible from the audience.

❑ Face the audience rather than the flip chart when talking.

❑ Avoid writing and speaking at the same time. If you record statements from the participants on a flip chart during a brainstorming, try to be quick or ask a participant to take notes while you facilitate. It is boring to watch someone taking notes.

Overhead slides

Overhead slides are plastic transparencies which are projected onto a screen by an overhead projector. You can prepare them by hand, writing with special indelible pens, or photocopy or print directly to the transparency. You can use them to provide outlines, main points and simple illustrations like on a flip chart. The advantage over the flip chart is that you can reproduce more complex graphs, diagrams or flow charts that would be difficult to copy out by hand. Considerable time can be saved by preparing the presentation on a computer using presentation software.

❑ Do not overload transparencies. Use the 'seven by seven' rule: no more than seven lines and no more than seven words per line.

❑ Include a title and page number on each transparency.

❑ Design transparencies so that people sitting in the back row can see them.

❑ Organize your transparencies in advance. There is nothing worse than shuffling through your transparencies in front of the room.

❑ Before starting a presentation, be sure that the overhead projector has been properly placed.

❑ Do not read from the slides; state the points with different terms.

❑ Do not give away everything you will say on the slides: the audience will read ahead rather than listen to you.

❑ When you speak, avoid standing in front of the screen. Sit next to the overhead projector and consult the slides on the machine, not on the screen – this way you will not turn your back to the audience.

❑ Turn off the projector when not in use.

❑ Know where to find extra bulbs for the projector (they are quite delicate and often burn out).

❑ Write directly on a blank as you would with a flip chart (important terms, or inputs from the audience, etc.).

Beamer – video projector

A video projector connected to a computer allows you to present visuals in the same way as you would with a transparency, using slides prepared with presentation software. Make sure you know how to connect the computer to the projector (ask for assistance from a technician if you are unsure). Allow time for the projector to warm up before the beginning of the session, so that the audience does not have to wait. The points on preparing materials for overhead projectors apply equally here.

Handouts

The purpose of handouts is multiple. They give the audience an anchor to help them remember what they have heard. They may also take the place of notes, or provide further information on the topic of the presentation, or provide graphs and diagrams that would be tedious to copy.

It is best to hand out materials at the end of the presentation. If you distribute material to participants just before your presentation, or while you speak, not only will the audience be distracted by the sound of shuffling paper, they will also start reading the handouts rather than listen to the lecture.

However, if your lecture includes a lot of numbers and charts that might be hard to see on the projector, you may choose to include these on handouts that you provide before the beginning of the lecture. Explain that you will be referring to these documents during your talk, and request that they not look at them until you ask them to. Make sure you know exactly which page to refer to when, or there will be confusion.

You may choose to hand out a bibliography. This provides a list of written works, either sources you used for your presentation or a selection of suggested reading for people who would like to learn more about the topic. You may also annotate the list with comments about the books.

The objective of the bibliography is to provide the information needed to find the work in a library or bookstore or on the Internet. The essential information you would provide for a book is:

❑ Author;

❑ Title (and subtitle);

❑ Place published (works in English often have different United States and United Kingdom editions);

❑ Publisher;

❑ Date published.

There are two ways of organizing the bibliography. The more classical approach is a list by author. The second option is to group works by topic, then list alphabetically by author. There are several standard formats for bibliographic entries of books, chapters in edited works, journal or newspaper articles, and websites. You will find more detailed guidelines on preparing bibliographies in most style manuals and many dictionaries.

Developing a role-play

Role-plays are a fantastic way to teach interactive skills and increase self-awareness. They are often used to teach 'people skills', such as sales or customer service, cross-cultural communications, and negotiation or mediation. They are also frequently used in leadership and management courses.

The origin of the role-play can be found in psychodrama, a form of therapy developed by the Viennese psychiatrist Levy Moreno (1889–1974). For Moreno, social life tends to lock individuals into a role, or a spectrum of roles. A personality is shaped by the sum of available roles the individual plays. As a result we develop role conformism: a mother behaves a certain way because she is expected to, as does a salesperson, and so on. Moreno believed that the role was not the core of the person but simply the behaviour of a person in a particular setting, in interaction with others. By putting people in situations where they could try out different roles, he hoped to expand their repertoire of roles and behaviours, and foster their personal growth.

While Moreno applied this discovery to his psychological practice, it has been proven equally effective in the training arena, where it is known as a role-play. The role-play puts learners in situations, and by making them experiment with new roles and new behaviours it allows them to expand their awareness.

The place of role-plays in training

Unlike purely technical skills, training in human relations (human resources, sales, management, and leadership) can happen only through a change of personal behaviour. The role-play provides an experience that may stimulate a change of behaviour, or raise awareness in the individual of how he or she communicates and relates to others.

A bit like in a case study, the role-play sets out a hypothetical situation that participants will have to analyse or interpret. They will have to impersonate one of the characters and act as if they were in the situation, according to what they know of similar real-life situations. Whereas in a case study the approach is purely intellectual and personal attitudes are not expressed, in the role-play spontaneous emotional and affective reactions are manifested. The role-play reveals both to actors and to viewers some of the fundamental assumptions, beliefs and attitudes that guide their behaviour in a defined situation. Once this awareness has been created, it is far easier to change attitudes, or practice new ones. The role-play can both reveal problematic behaviours and help modify them.

Role-plays have to be used with prudence and respect for the trainees, since they can reveal a lot about the personality and intimate beliefs of individuals. Debriefing makes many people uncomfortable since they feel they are being personally judged. It is therefore important to give feedback tactfully.

Typology of role-plays

Several types of role-plays are used in professional training.

The directed role-play

The trainer chooses the theme and designs the scenario from a real-life professional situation, with clearly stated objectives (sell more products, obtain a raise, etc.). The scenario describes the context and summarizes the role of each player succinctly. The first option is to leave it up to the participants to improvise their roles as they feel. The second option is to write the dialogues out and ask the participants to give voice to them with their own gestures and attitudes.

Group-centred role-play

If a typical or problematic situation arises during the training session (conflicts or sexist attitudes, for example), the trainer may use it as the basis for a role-play scenario. In pairs or in triplets, participants play out the situation in front of the group. This leads to discussion of how the situation was handled, how it could play out better, and ultimately to the resolution of the conflict through more awareness and communication.

Vignettes

In these quick, four- to five-minute role-plays, participants present a situation with gestures and dialogues that they have composed, based on a scenario provided by the trainer. Vignettes can be very entertaining, but to maintain the energy level they need to follow each other quickly.

The sketch

A sketch is a short play. The participants usually write the sketch themselves, based on a situation or objective defined by the trainer. The trainer may participate in the sketch as well.

Observing and debriefing role-plays

As we stated earlier, the power of any role-play is in the observation and debriefing phase. It is worth preparing this part of the role-play thoroughly. Providing an observation sheet on which the observers record their impressions is a way of focusing observation on the training objectives at hand. The observation sheet should be prepared in advance to fit the role-play situations. It has to direct observation to measurable and objective criteria such as gestures, postures, vocabulary, language and tone of voice.

Figure 16	Sample observation sheet		
Observed points	**Positive elements**	**To be improved**	**Techniques to apply**

According to the subject of the role-play, the evaluation sheet has to be more or less precise.

There are several ways to organize observation.

- ❑ **Designate a member of a sub-group as the observer.** If you have divided into groups of three or more, one of them will act as an observer. Observers receive clear instructions on what they should be watching for. Participants are then spread around the room and take turns within their subgroups to perform the role-play.

- ❑ **Have the entire group observe**. The players take turns coming to the front of the room while the rest of the group observes. Although more intimidating, this approach creates one single experience for the group, which can serve as a reference point during the programme.

- ❑ **Record role-plays on video.** Players act out the role-play in a separate room, and are filmed. The video can be viewed 'live' from another room on closed-circuit TV, or can be viewed later by the trainer, the players themselves or the entire group. The advantage of the video is that it is a neutral mirroring tool: the impact of seeing oneself can be much greater than that of having others tell us what they saw. The disadvantage is that it is technically more complex to implement.

Some tips on using video:

- ❑ Do not record on video unless you plan ample time to review the video. If you fail to do so, expect participants to say 'what about the video?'

- ❑ The players themselves will be most interested in watching themselves on the video. Do not inflict long observation sessions on the entire group.

- ❑ If you do wish to show filmed role-plays to the group, select passages that will be of greatest interest to them, either by editing the video or timing it so that you can fast-forward to the points you have chosen beforehand.

- ❑ People love to see themselves on film, so make the video available to them for their own use during the course.

- ❑ Being filmed can be inhibiting. Put participants at ease and explain the purpose of the filming.

- ❑ Unless you are conducting public speaking or train-the-trainers workshops, do not hand out copies of the video.

- ❑ Check the equipment prior to using it to avoid time-consuming glitches and last-minute adjustments.

Preparing a role-play

Three types of documents must be created to offer role-plays as a method of teaching:

The overall scenario provides the context of the role-play. It describes the case in detail. If the role-play is a sales negotiation between a company and a potential client, the scenario will describe the product, the type of client the company already has, the quality of the production, the circumstances of the meeting, and the expectations of both parties.

Scenarios can vary in length. If the role-play is expected to last 15 to 30 minutes, the scenario should be no longer than a page.

The **role sheet** describes the protagonists of the role-play. It provides a profile of the characters, their history and objectives. It should not be a full description of a personality, but should give just enough information for the participant to interpret the character. In many situations, it is perfectly feasible to have participants play their own real-life role. In this case, the role-play veers towards simulation. The closer to reality the situation is, the more useful the role-play will be for the participants. On the other hand, the closer the situation is to one that the participants know well, the more they will challenge the trainer's recommendations and coaching. They will make comments like 'In my experience, that's not how it is', 'I would never do that', 'My client would never react like that', and so on.

The role sheets (one per character) should never exceed half a page in a 15- to 30-minute role-play.

The third document is the **observation sheet** described above, which is used to record observations on the role-play.

How to introduce a role-play

Present the exercise and its objectives. You could introduce a negotiation role-play by saying:

> *We are going to do a role-play simulating the 'final sales negotiation between company A and company B'. The objective is to try to apply some techniques for 'how to close a deal'. The role-play will last 15 minutes. You will be given 20 minutes alone to prepare your role and define your arguments and your objectives. You will have an observer in each group. The role of the observer will be to capture some of the key moments of the simulation and provide feedback to each person using the framework in the observation sheet provided.*

How to manage and conclude a role-play

It is best not to intervene during the role-play. If the participants stop the play because of laughter or because they question the rules, you can involve the larger group in redefining the rules or in refocusing the activity.

The debriefing stage will be more efficient if the observation sheets are well designed. However, before soliciting observations from the audience or observers, let the players give their impressions and reactions to the role-play or the character they interpreted. When both players and observers have spoken, the trainer can synthesize the comments.

When giving feedback, first talk about the positive points, and then give criticism. Follow on any criticism with suggestions for improvement. You can also let the players read the comments made by their peers on the observation sheets.

If you feel the need during debriefing to restate some of the learning points of the role-play, make reference either to a cognitive model or to an input. Try to stay at the level of the group when making those comments, and find a balance between positive and critical inputs. Thank participants for their participation and efforts.

The role of the facilitator/trainer

The role of facilitator is to help the process flow smoothly so that the learning objectives are met. He or she does what is necessary to facilitate self-expression, positive interaction and learning within the group. The facilitator gives comments based on the content, and does not stand in judgement of individuals and their ideas, opinions or attitudes.

To ensure that interactions are open and positive, the trainer must create an environment of trust. Judgemental and critical attitudes are not conducive to trust. Often critical comments from observers can be defused by restating them in a more positive, neutral or constructive way. Participants will then follow the trainer's example. Furthermore, the trainer should strictly avoid taking sides.

The facilitator guides the process by:

❑ Designating people to speak;
❑ Making sure everyone participates;
❑ Understanding the group's reactions;
❑ Restating when necessary;
❑ Mirroring;
❑ Keeping track of time;
❑ Synthesizing comments;
❑ Drawing out the learning points.

Tips on facilitating role-plays

As you can see, facilitating role-plays requires a great deal of tact and objectivity: the players are being judged in part on their personal beliefs and attitudes expressed in the play, and can be sensitive about criticism. The way you facilitate can do a lot to ensure the discussion engages the entire group without becoming destabilizing to individuals.

Start by thanking the entire group. Solicit reactions from the players first. Ask them:

❑ What were their feelings during the role-play?
❑ What were their intentions and their objectives?
❑ What was revealed during this exercise?
❑ How did they experience the relationship between the players during the role-play?
❑ What were the phases of the role-play? Can they describe them?

The facilitator will then turn to the group and ask:

❑ What did they observe?
❑ What feedback can they give back to the players?
❑ Do they have the same perceptions as the players about what happened?
❑ Does what happened fit with what was planned in the preparation?
❑ How would they have played the role differently?

Only after this point does the facilitator analyse the play in his or her own terms.

The debriefing of a role-play should achieve these four objectives:

❑ Raise awareness of the difficulty of the particular situation and the roles as they were described in the brief.

❑ Raise awareness of the interpretation that each person gave to his or her role and to the situation.

❑ Highlight the variety of interpretations that could be given to the same situation.

❑ Analyse the mental processes which shaped the attitude of each player, their personal reactions, their interpretations, the way they set priorities and what they dismissed or ignored.

Organizing the training space

The way a room is set up is also a communication tool. It is the first impression that participants will get of the course: the training room layout 'sets the tone' of the course. The layout has the ability to enhance communication or on the contrary hinder it.

Two basic principles guide the choice of a layout:

❑ The participants should always see whoever is speaking. Check the lighting, and do not have speakers stand in front of windows. Place overhead projectors and flip charts so that everyone can see them.

❑ The layout should be modified according to the task that is given to the participants. A set-up does not have to be permanent; you may change it from one day to the next.

Figure 17 suggests two alternatives, the first a traditional classroom set-up, the second allowing for more interactivity. It is best to change during long breaks (such as lunch or in the evening).

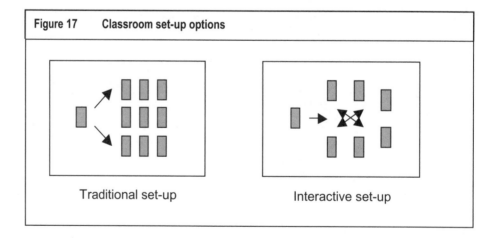

Figure 17	Classroom set-up options

Traditional set-up   Interactive set-up

There are traditional ways of organizing a room as well as non-traditional ones.

Several pointers help in planning the layout.

❑ Will the teaching method lean more towards presentations or facilitation?

❑ Will participants need to interact with each other in small groups or larger groups?

❑ Will there be many formal presentations requiring an overhead projector or video equipment?

❑ Will participants need to take notes?

❑ Will they be involved in experiential exercises?

Depending on the type of participation sought, different layouts will be appropriate, as shown in figure 18.

Figure 18   Choice of classroom layout

Type of participation	Layout
Listening You provide all the inputs, or call on speakers to present. This is a conference setting, where the speaker may additionally stand on a platform. This set-up may remind the participants of their school days. In an amphitheatre hall the effect is very imposing.	
Exchange You wish to favour exchanges between participants. Two layouts are suggested: the U-style maintains tables for written work (note that people sitting at the very end of the table do not see the others). If tables are not essential, you can sit people in a circle or oval. The chairs can then be moved again easily into a new configuration for small group activities.	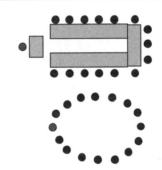
Collective work If the objective is for everyone in the group to work together on a project, the best option is to sit them all at the same table in such a way that everyone can see everyone else. These layouts put the trainer at the same level as the participants, suggesting a role as a facilitator rather than a leader.	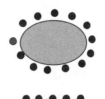
Individual or small group work Some programmes require a lot of small groups to discuss, work on case studies, solve problems or reach resolutions on issues. This arrangement offers the maximum flexibility and rotation of participants, but it also allows everyone to listen to the trainer's presentations and debriefings.	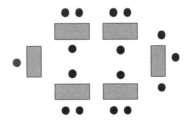

Dealing with difficult situations

Just as groups can be a source of learning for their participants, they can also be a source of resistance to learning (we mentioned barriers to learning in module 1). When tensions and conflict arise, it can be a sign that the trainer is not managing the group well. It can also be a symptom of motivational or organizational problems. Indeed, sometimes participants' negative feelings are justified: you need to hear them out and help them find mutually beneficial solution.

Moderating conflict

Some of the common conflict situations are outlined below, along with suggestions on how you might handle them. The common theme of all these strategies is listening and facilitating to help the group find solutions to whatever is keeping it from functioning as a positive learning environment.

Situation/justification	Attitude of the trainer
The group is resisting from the first hour of the programme. Justification: *We have been forced to come; we have not requested training; we don't see the utility of it, etc.*	❑ Discuss the resistance and its cause right away. As long as you do not speak about the issues that are draining the energy of the group, you will be unable to make any progress. ❑ Listen actively. ❑ Help them analyse the situation. ❑ Ask the trainees what would make them feel the training is worthwhile. ❑ Agree to modify certain parts of the programme (keeping in mind the contractual objectives). It helps if trainers are responsible for the content and allowed to take such decisions. ❑ Ask them to commit to the new conditions that you have negotiated with them.
Justification: *The previous training/consulting firm betrayed us, informed management of what we said in class, etc. Why should we trust you?*	❑ Remind them that professional ethics require the trainer to respect their confidentiality. ❑ Suggest that the group lay out the rules they would like you to follow in this regard. ❑ Ask one or two members of the group to be the guardians of confidentiality, making sure all notes are erased at the end of the course.
Various other fears about the training.	❑ Ask them to formulate their fears very precisely. ❑ De-dramatize the fears. ❑ Restate the purpose of the course as it was sold to the company or to the participants.
The group is lethargic and does not get involved.	❑ Reformulate the attitude you observe, 'I notice that you are not very motivated …' ❑ Question them about their lack of motivation. ❑ Reframe the objectives of the session, or of the exercise. ❑ Change pace and mode of teaching or take a break. ❑ Ask a provocative question to start a discussion.

Situation/justification	Attitude of the trainer
The group is stalled and is not progressing.	❑ Clarify the objectives of the task. ❑ Get them to tell you why they are stuck. ❑ Provide explanations and clarification. ❑ Change teaching methods or group organization: for instance, go from small groups back to a large group, or switch to lecturing mode.
Participants are talking to each other rather than listening.	❑ Do not react too quickly; see if the conversations will end by themselves. ❑ Stop talking and wait for silence. ❑ If the talking continues, ask the speakers if they have something they would like to share with the rest of the group. ❑ If the problem persists, it may be a sign of lack of interest: the sequence of the programme may be at fault or the participants may be bored and/or feel that they are not learning anything new. In either case you should not fail to question them about what is causing the problem.
The group refuses to continue because a member of management or an outside guest has entered the room.	❑ Ask the 'outsider' to explain the purpose of his or her presence. ❑ Ask the person to leave for a few minutes, and discuss with the group the reason for their behaviour. You may find a way to get the group to agree on some conditions, such as confidentiality and discretion, which would make the presence of the outsider acceptable.

The group is aggressive.
 	
There is conflict between two participants.
	❑ Use the mirroring technique known as DEPE:
	    Describe the situation.
	    Express your opinion and your feeling.
	    Propose a solution.
	    Evaluate the positive consequences.
	❑ Understand the reasons.
	❑ Concentrate on facts and not people.
	❑ Refuse to contribute to the emotional build-up.
	❑ Moderate without moralizing or accusing.
	❑ If the conflict persists, stop the course and ask for the most aggressive members to leave.
	❑ Listen to the perceptions of each party.
	❑ Establish rules of good communication and respect (speak calmly, personally and not in the name of the group, listen, do not interrupt, etc.).
	❑ Search for a solution to be able to continue the training.
	❑ Ask the participants to be accountable for any further disruption.
	❑ Reach an agreement to continue the training.

There is competition between a group of trainees and the trainer.	❑ Never contest what they say, but clearly express your position; give examples, references, name authors, research, etc. ❑ Avoid confrontation on non-essential issues. ❑ Engage the group in thinking with you. ❑ Listen, praise, congratulate, give feedback. ❑ Do not exacerbate the competition by trying to look brilliant.

Managing difficult personalities

Just as groups can disrupt a training session and make it difficult for anyone to learn anything, so can certain individuals. A person can become difficult because of extreme character traits, which make it impossible for the person to get along with the group or go along with the training relationship. You should be aware that:

❑ A difficult personality has not chosen to be difficult, and is not doing so just to spite the trainer. Therefore the trainer should be tolerant and give the person the benefit of the doubt.

❑ Any moralizing attitude will fail.

❑ Training is also a means to increase self-awareness, even in difficult situations.

❑ Some personality types are more likely to cause difficulty in the classroom. They are:
  – The worried;
  – The rigid and picky;
  – The suspicious;
  – The narcissistic;
  – The reserved;
  – The passive-aggressive;
  – The theatrical;
  – The authoritarian;
  – The talkative;
  – The timid.

Handling each of these personality types takes skill, tact and psychology. It helps if you think about what motivates the disruptive behaviour and how you can inhibit it (for instance by channelling the problematic personality trait into a more positive expression). Here are some more general tips on how to handle both general situations of conflict and problems with individuals:

❑ Speak honestly so as to provide the opportunity for the person in front of you to speak honestly.

❑ Behind each difficult personality there is an unmet need. Within the context of the training, the trainer can identify this need, and perhaps satisfy it totally or partially.

❑ One must be able to say 'no' to the behaviour but 'yes' to the person, refusing deviant behaviour but maintaining the relationship with the participant.

❑ Identify the source of the conflict and not just the symptom. The trainer must try to understand and explore the reason for conflict or aggressive behaviour.

❑ Adopt a good listening attitude. Treat the participants as responsible adults and equals, but if the conflict persists do not fear to be firm.

❑ Always be very aware of your own attitudes towards the trainees with whom you are in conflict.

Module 6

Managing training programmes

The trainer as manager

In the previous modules you learned about the methods, skills, tools and techniques that will enhance your effectiveness as a trainer. However, all this will be useless unless you also develop your skills as a manager. Indeed, delivering a training course requires extensive planning and people-management. The most articulate presentation will be thrown into disarray if the trainees all arrive late because they were not told how to find the classroom. A wonderful new case study that took time and effort to prepare will fall flat if you did not bring enough handouts for everyone.

This is neither the most creative nor the most enjoyable part of the job. However, the benefits of thorough planning and preparation will be felt further down the line, as fewer glitches and crises to deal with during the course allow you to focus on the delivery.

In addition to logistical planning skills you will have to develop your ability to manage people. You will often be coordinating with other trainers. If you work for a training company, you may be asked to manage a pool of in-house or freelance trainers, or called on to train new trainers. Project management tools will help you manage resources and meet deadlines.

Finally, no course is complete without an evaluation phase. Evaluations give you precious feedback. They tell you whether you have reached your objectives, whether the trainees have achieved their goals, and suggest ways to improve the content, form and delivery of the course.

In this module we will address the following topics:

- ❑ The venue;
- ❑ Logistics;
- ❑ Knowing your audience;
- ❑ Evaluation;
- ❑ Managing trainers;
- ❑ Accreditation.

The venue

It is crucial to have contact ahead of time with the venue where the course will take place. Many courses are held in hotels or conference facilities because they offer meeting rooms, catering and accommodation, thus minimizing the number of service providers you need to deal with. You are a client of the venue where you organize the course. They need to learn how to best serve you. To make sure this is the case, you need to establish a personal relationship with the venue manager. Identify yourself on arrival and take the time to sit down with him or her in order to explain your needs and requests. Provide a programme that includes a precise schedule for coffee breaks, lunch and conference room usage, particularly if you plan evening sessions.

Similarly, do not forget to thank the manager before leaving, and share any feedback about your stay. It is worth keeping track of good venues, and it might be useful to keep a little folder on each conference centre or hotel you have used.

If the client has chosen the venue, make sure you visit it or receive enough information before giving your agreement. There is nothing worse than a room that turns out to be too small for the number of participants, or is dark or cramped, especially when you have to spend more than a couple days in it. If this is the case, you should explain to the client why the proposed venue is unsuitable and suggest a different one.

Rooms

Depending on the course design, you may need to break the group up into small rooms for group work or discussion groups. Conversely, for dynamic experiential exercises or simulations you will need a large of space. A multi-function conference room like those found in many hotels has partitions which can be added or remove to change the configuration of the room. This is the ideal, but is not always available, so the size of the group and your logistical needs should be clearly defined to help you choose rooms. Beware of poorly equipped hotel conference rooms that are sandwiched between the dining room and a bar: these are a nightmare to teach in, and you should turn them down outright.

Equipment

It is always good to come well equipped so that you do not depend on the venue for services that they may not provide. Plan for extra photocopies of articles, scenarios and training material. Ask in advance if the venue stocks extra light bulbs for the overhead projector, or bring one yourself. Similarly, request extra flip chart paper in case you run out. Make sure you bring chalk, indelible pens or whiteboard markers, as needed.

If you have prepared your presentation on the computer and intend to use the video projector, it is best to bring your own computer and your own projector, if you own one. Make sure that you know how to use the projector provided at the venue, and check you have all the cables, plugs, and so on. Bring a long extension cord; you never know where power sources are located.

Coffee breaks

Coffee breaks can sometimes be served in the conference room itself. Although this can be quite convenient, be aware that waiters setting up the coffee table may disrupt the end of the session, just as the cleaning away of the coffee things may delay the beginning of the next session.

Lunch

You might have planned for lunch to last no more than an hour, so as to get the most out of the day. In many cultures, however, lunch is a long, leisurely affair; you should check with the banquet manager or the caterer whether a short lunch is feasible. It is part of your job to ask participants if they have any particular dietary requirements and to inform the hotel of them.

In some cultures, it is normal that wine or beer be served for lunch. If you prefer that no alcoholic beverages be served, specify it to the caterer.

Accommodation

If the course extends over several days and requires all or some of the participants to spend the night in a hotel, you should organize a lodging package. The usual arrangement is that participants pay for their room and board. However, if the training is organized for a single company, they may opt to put everyone's expenses on a master bill. You should be informed of what this master bill includes (just room and lunch, or drinks and dinner as well), so that you can remind participants of these details in the first session of the course. On the last day, let the trainees know by what time they should check out and where they can store their luggage.

Prior to the course

There are many things to keep in mind when organizing the venue. Here are the main ones. You will also find the preparation checklist provided in appendix III helpful.

❑ Provide clear information on the set-up of the room (see module 5 for a discussion of the different options for class layout).

❑ Check they have the equipment you need to deliver the course:

– Overhead projector;

– Flip charts;

– Screen;

– Video projector;

– Connection cables, multiple plugs.

❑ Request a table with water and glasses.

❑ Request an extra table for setting up your material.

❑ Provide a schedule of your programme with clear indication of time of coffee breaks and lunch.

❑ Request the name of a contact person at the venue (and the times when they are available).

❑ Inform yourself of the availability of a photocopy machine and computer.

When arriving at the venue

❑ Locate toilets, exits, conference rooms you will use.

❑ Inform yourself of the availability of staff (from whom you may ask for help with photocopies or other miscellaneous needs).

❑ Obtain a key to the conference room.

❑ Request cleaning of the room at certain times during the day.

❑ Check the set-up of the main room and any break-up rooms used.

❑ Make sure water and glasses are available.

❑ Check paper on flip charts, number of flip charts, and markers. If you are using a whiteboard check there is the sponge to clean it and erasable markers.

❑ Verify all equipment, particularly all electronic equipment.

❑ Understand lights and heating or ventilation system.

❑ Learn how to open windows.

On departure

❑ Make sure you clear away all the materials and handouts left.

❑ Thank and give feedback to the venue manager.

❑ Return all keys and make sure rooms are orderly.

Logistics

When participants arrive at the course venue, you want everything to flow as smoothly as possible. There are several things you can do ahead of time to make sure that participants know where to go and what is expected of them, feel welcomed and well informed, and receive all the course materials they need. They will be thankful to the organizer for thinking of all the little details that ensure that the course runs well.

Information package

Participants should receive an information package or confirmation letter prior to the programme. If the course is organized for employees of a single company, the company may take on much of the planning work, including the information package. However information is most often prepared and sent by the trainer or the training company two to three weeks before the course begins.

This information package should include a welcome letter and attachments:

❑ The title of the course.

❑ The key learning objectives.

❑ A programme schedule.

❑ A short biography of the trainer(s).

❑ A list of participants.

❑ The address and phone number of the venue.

❑ The time when participants are expected to arrive.

❑ The dress code: casual or business.

❑ Any registration fees that will be payable on site and the preferred mode of payment.

❑ Other practical details: transport, hotel check-in, special dietary requirements.

In some executive seminars, the list of participants includes a photograph of the trainees and a short biography of each person. This is expensive to do, but you could consider it for a small group. A good photocopier is essential for rendering photographs.

Welcome desk

Arrange for a sign to be placed in the hotel or conference centre reception area to direct people to the conference room.

If the group is large, some form of registration or check-in needs to be in place. Set up a desk in an open area close to the conference room, where you can welcome attendees, checking their name against your list as they arrive. This is a good time to hand them a badge, a detailed programme, training folder, handouts, etc. The welcome desk is the first impression the participants will get from the course, so it is important that it be well organized. It is usually staffed by hotel or venue staff, so trainers can concentrate on other last-minute details.

If you do not have a welcome desk, write a welcome message on a flip chart and hand the badges and training folders to the participants as they arrive in the room.

Badges

There are several models of badge:

- ❑ Plastic clip-on badge.
- ❑ Plastic badge with safety pin.
- ❑ Badges hanging on a string to be worn around the neck.
- ❑ Sticky tags to glue onto shirts or dresses.

The name tag inserted into the badge can include full name or title and last name, position and company. If it is a very informal course, you can simply have participants write their first names with markers on sticky labels. This approach can encourage an informal atmosphere, where position and rank are de-emphasized. However, you should choose the level of formality that is most appropriate to the culture you are working in.

If participants are seated behind tables, it might be nice to also plan for name cards, which are easy to make out of A5-size heavy card folded in half. The name should be written in large type, so that the trainer can read them from the front of the room and call people by name.

List of participants

You should prepare a list of participants including name, title, and company or organization for checking attendance on the first day. This list will also be appreciated by trainees for keeping in touch with other participants after the programme. In this perspective, it is useful to include telephone numbers and e-mail addresses. Quite often, the participants list needs to be corrected; keep a copy on your computer so that you can make changes to it before handing it to participants at the end of the course.

Folders

Handouts are best organized in a folder or ring binder. This should be a standard size that fits easily into a briefcase. Another option often used by training companies is to hand out a light canvas briefcase to hold the handouts, notes and any other documents the trainee collects. The briefcase can be printed with the name of the course and the logo of the client company or the training company.

At the beginning of the course, this folder will hold only what is necessary for the introduction (practical details, lists) and first session. It is best to give handouts when they are needed rather than ahead of time.

Some simple guidelines to follow when planning the folder:

- ❑ Imagine yourself using this folder – think of what you would want in it.
- ❑ Don't try to include everything.
- ❑ Include a notepad for taking notes. In the learning process, notes are more important than printed handouts.
- ❑ Make sure the folder is large enough to add documents.
- ❑ If the course is organized for a single company, you may want to have their logo, as well as the training company's logo, address and phone number, printed on the folder.
- ❑ If you are using ring binders make sure all the documents you are distributing have the right number of holes punched in them already or bring a hole puncher with you.

During the training sessions

Timing

Participants should always know where they are in the course schedule. Either you make reference to the schedule you have distributed or you show on the slide where you are in the programme. They should know how long the session will last and what is the next step or the next break. Strict time management during the programme is essential. This does not mean that you cannot overrun a session, but it is important to let people know if you are doing so.

Keep your timing punctual and request that participants do so as well. When you send them on breaks or for group work, give them a time to return. Call them back from break or circulate among groups to remind them when their preparation time is up.

Similarly, tell them precisely how much time they have to make a presentation, and let them know in advance when they are reaching the end of their time. Keep the timing strict.

Some trainers come with a clock, which they set in front of their desk; others come with a kitchen timer or even an hourglass.

The emphasis on punctuality should be clear from the beginning of the session. There are some tricks to making sure people arrive on time. If the participants know each other well, you may put latecomers on the spot by requesting them to tell a joke in front of everyone, for instance. Or you may start your session with a short quiz and call on the latecomers to answer.

Handouts

Your handout materials should be well organized, so that you know exactly what to distribute when. You should choose when to distribute handouts based on how they will be used. If they are to serve as a reminder of the content of a presentation, they should be given after the presentation. If they are needed for a practical exercise, case study, role-play or evaluation, then they should be given out beforehand.

Lay handouts out in front of each participant's seat during the breaks. When the session resumes, explain what the materials are for, and when trainees should look at them. Usually people want to pick up the handouts and look through them immediately; this not only diverts their attention from what you are saying, but also produces a distracting background noise. It you want them to wait before reading the handouts, say so.

If your presentation uses overheads or slides, let the participants know that a copy of the slides will be handed out later. This is especially practical if the slides contain a lot of data, definition and complex acronyms. Participants tend to interrupt you to request time to transcribe important information, which slows down the presentation. Anticipate this need by announcing that they will get a printed copy of the slides after the presentation. They will then be better able to concentrate on what you are saying.

You can also distribute copies of your slides before you start the presentation, and suggest that they take notes directly on the handouts. We suggest you print four slides per page with room for notes: detailed slides will still be legible, but will take up less space on paper.

The room

The room (or rooms) in which the course is held should always be kept clean and tidy. The room should give an impression of order and cleanliness. Request that venue staff clean and air the room during long breaks.

❑ Water pitchers should be replenished, and glasses changed;

❑ Garbage bins should be emptied;

❑ Papers should be stacked;

❑ Your desk should be tidy;

❑ Your handout materials should be organized;

❑ Chairs and tables should be put back in place;

❑ Flip charts should be refilled and in place.

Audio-visual equipment

You need to know how to use all audio-visual equipment well. The trainer who struggles for minutes at a time to connect the computer to the projector, or starts off a session by placing a transparency upside down on the overhead projector, makes a very poor impression. So check with a technician if you are unsure how to work the equipment, and practise until you get it right.

Avoid leaving the overhead projector on when not in use, as the light is distracting and has a tendency to overheat. Learn how to adjust the focus of the image.

When using slides or overhead transparencies, do not turn your back to the audience. Read the slides on your computer screen or the overhead glass.

It can be handy to have a laser pointer to pick out details of the slides. With transparencies you can use a thin stick or pen as a pointer.

If you are using microphones:

❑ Learn how to turn them on and off;

❑ Test them beforehand and check the volume of your voice;

❑ If you move around, watch your position so that you do not produce the loud whistling caused by feedback from speakers to the microphone;

❑ Bring extra batteries if you are using a cordless microphone;

❑ Learn how to use the mixing table.

If you are using video:

❑ Make sure the video is connected and you know how to turn the system on;

❑ Test the equipment and preview your video on it;

❑ Wind the video forward or back to the starting point;

❑ Test the sound;

❑ Position the screen or TV set so that everyone can see it;

❑ Learn how to stop and pause the video.

Group work

A lot of time can be lost setting up group work. You can avoid this by forming groups ahead of time and providing a list of groups and participants on a slide, overhead transparency or flip chart.

If you ask the participants to form groups themselves, give them a short deadline so that it does not take too long. You may also form groups randomly by counting off: to form three groups you number the participants, by calling out 'One, two, three; one, two, three', as you point at each in turn. The 'ones' then form a first group, the 'twos' a second and the 'threes' a third. This is a good tactic for mixing up the group, since people tend to sit next to friends.

Before forming groups decide:

❑ How the groups will be organized;

❑ What materials they will need to work together, such as Post-its, handouts, etc.;

❑ Where they will work;

❑ What materials should be provided in the workspace (flip charts, whiteboard, etc.);

❑ Time allocated to the group activity;

❑ When the groups should report back.

When people work in groups you need to provide them with a clear assignment. No matter how clear you have been with your instructions in plenary, it is always worth circulating between the groups to answer questions and make sure that they have understood the assignment and are on task. Let the group know where they can find you if they need your help.

If the process you are using is new to you, it might be worth staying longer in a group to gain some insight into how the process is working.

Knowing your audience

Prior to starting a programme, you should have a fairly good idea of the audience you will be facing: their background, their expectations, their experience, and the company or companies they work for. This will help you target the course to the audience.

Part of your preparation includes learning a bit about the company they work for, what they do and why they are attending the course. This information should help you adjust the examples and the practical application of your teaching so that they are relevant to the trainees. Similarly, knowing what they do will allow you to call upon their expertise and their knowledge.

One way you can learn more about the group is by getting them to fill in a questionnaire. In appendix IV we provide two standard pre-course questionnaires that should help you gather useful information.

Sometimes this information can be useful when you create small groups, allowing you to put participants from the same types of industry together, or on the contrary provide a mix of knowledge and expertise.

The questionnaires in appendix IV are examples; you can add any type of questions you consider appropriate and useful.

Managing trainers

Selecting the right trainer for the programme you have planned and designed is crucial to ensuring the quality of the delivery. These are the situations you are likely to face:

❑ You developed the contact with the client, you have designed the course and you will deliver it.

❑ Your training company has a permanent staff of trainers, and you can choose from a pool of people whom you know and have trained.

❑ Your training company works with freelance trainers, who are called on if and when they are needed.

The first situation is, of course, the easiest to deal with, since you have full control of the programme, know the client and know what your capabilities are.

The second and third situations require more management skills, as you will have to deal with staff you may or may not know very well. You will be in charge of briefing trainers on what is expected of them, and you may be called on to train these trainers before they can go out and train others.

Training and briefing trainers

Briefing trainers

Whether you are using permanent staff or freelance trainers, you need to give the trainer some key information about the client(s) he or she will be working with, such as:

❑ What the client does;

❑ What their position in the market is;

❑ Who their competitors are;

❑ The key contact people in the client company: their perception of the course, their influence within the company and on the training project;

❑ Training programmes the company has carried out in the past;

❑ The history of the programme development (if it is tailor-made), how the project came about, etc.

Just as it is important to provide the trainer with information about the client before the course, it is also quite crucial that all key information collected during the course be transferred back to the training organization. In big training companies, there are salespeople who act as account managers, contacting clients and then facilitating information collection before, during and after the course.

Training the trainers

If a training programme is new, you will probably need to train trainers to deliver it. For a three-day programme, trainers normally receive nine days of training. This may seem like a lot, especially if the trainers are experienced and have delivered similar courses in the past. However, skimping on training for the trainers can have disastrous consequences for the quality of the course.

'Train the trainers' programmes require thorough preparation and planning. The nine days of training for delivering a three-day programme would be organized like this:

❑ Days 1 and 2: the trainers follow the course programme from the point of view of the participant, with the difference that three days of training are condensed into two.

❑ Days 3 and 4: the programme is studied session by session so that trainers understand content, read materials, learn tools, and practise simulations, case studies and demonstrations.

❑ Days 5 and 6: rehearse presentations, introduction of exercises, debriefings.

❑ Days 7 and 8: rehearse entire programme.

❑ Day 9: review logistical issues and client profiles.

Train-the-trainers programmes can be quite dynamic. They are definitely a privileged learning moment for the trainers, who get to practise, rehearse and receive feedback from their peers or from a senior trainer. If you are involved in a long training programme such as the one outlined above, you may wish to include a small team-building exercise to reinforce the trainers' sense of belonging.

Pilot programmes

When delivering a new programme, it can be helpful to test it on an audience that will give you reliable critical feedback: this is known as a pilot programme. The feedback will then help fine-tune the content, methods, speed, tools, etc. The audience can be made up of trainers and observers, or anyone who has influence or decision-making power in the company or the organization.

There are several ways to organize a pilot programme:

❑ You deliver the programme as if it were for the target audience. At the end of the session, you conduct an extensive feedback session.

❑ You spend some time debriefing after each module. This is a good method for long programmes, but the audience may become a bit schizophrenic, not knowing when they are expected to act like participants and when like evaluators.

❑ You deliver the programme to the actual target audience, but invite several observers to sit through it and take notes. After each module, or at end of the course you sit down with the observers and receive their feedback.

In addition to providing feedback to improve the course, pilots can be useful also in training a new trainer or persuading a reluctant client. If you expect the course to be delivered many times, you may include all the trainers who will be involved in the project as the audience.

The feedback on a pilot must be done both verbally, at the end of the session, and in writing, after a week. This extra time allows observers to develop deeper insight on the experience.

If you have a series of programmes rolling out simultaneously, anticipate running the pilot two or three weeks before the first real delivery so that you have plenty of time to adjust the programme design, materials and so on.

Trainer's manual

Just as participants receive a participant folder, trainers need to have a training manual to work with. The manual guides them through the delivery of the course. Having a good manual for a programme also ensures that the programme will be replicable many times with a minimum of variation. If you are responsible for preparing this manual you should pay attention to the following guidelines:

❑ Describe exercises thoroughly: highlight debriefing points, mention alternative activities, provide examples and illustrations.

❑ Do not write out lectures in full, but provide main points supporting data.

❑ Prepare lectures in bullet points and include the presentation slides or transparencies.

❑ Prepare some questions to ask the trainees, and the answers.

A copy of all the course handouts should be included in the trainer's manual.

Keep a master copy of all course documents in the office. If the course evolves over time, keep a master copy for every version, in order to track the changes. This, of course, requires a fairly well-organized filing system.

Project management

As we have seen so far, delivering a training programme can be quite a complex task, requiring you to keep track of numerous small logistical details, as well as plan delivery, train and manage trainers, and so on. Methods of project management are extremely useful in putting order into the preparation and delivery of the course by prioritizing, timing and allocating responsibilities for tasks. A good project visualization tool is the Gantt chart.

Gantt charts

The Gantt chart is like a calendar that lists all tasks required to prepare, launch and deliver a project. The Gantt chart shows when to start a task, when to deliver it and the number of days required. It allows you to plan resources and set deadlines for each step of the process. You can quickly assess the number of workdays needed and use this estimate to calculate your costs.

Figure 19	Simplified Gantt chart					
Name of project: Project manager: Date of chart:						
Task	**January**	**February**	**March**	**April**	**May**
Analyse request	1 day				
Feasibility study	3 days				
Course concept	1 day				
Approval of course concept	*31 Jan*				
First draft of course		5 days			
Approval of course		*19 Feb*			
Prepare material			8 days		
Client approval			2 days		
Select trainers		*20 Feb*			
Train-the-trainer preparation			4 days		
Train the trainers			7 days		
Run pilot programme				2 days	
Approve final design				*21 Apr*	
Launch – 1st programme					*1 May*
2nd programme					*15 May*

Planners

Coordination between trainers and within a training company can be greatly facilitated by using a simple wall planner. The wall planner has a line for each trainer, and columns for days of the week or weeks in the month. In each cell of the planner you indicate where that trainer will be on that particular day, and what course he or she is delivering. You can use the planner to see at a glance where your trainers or consultants are and what they are doing. You can also circulate a printed copy of the planner to all the trainers and consultants.

Hiring trainers

If you are working with freelance trainers or consultants you will have to agree to the terms of a contract for the time you will work together. Hiring freelance staff is a cost-effective way to employ people as you need them, especially in the start-up phase of a new training or consulting business. However, managing freelance trainers can be complex: the relationship can sour quickly if the freelancer fails to provide the quality of service you expect, acts unethically, or argues over the terms of payment. To be fair, the responsibility is sometimes on the side of the employer, who may have not briefed the trainer sufficiently or left some terms of the contract vague.

Prior to hiring a freelancer, you need to clarify the terms of the collaboration so that there is no chance of misunderstanding. The relationship with a freelance trainer is a business partnership. The trainer is being paid for his or her expertise, but he or she is also deriving satisfaction from using that expertise and from belonging to a challenging and dynamic professional network. As in any business relationship, communication is the key to building a solid partnership with the freelance trainer, one in which he or she will be proactive and dynamic.

In the contract with the freelance trainer you should agree on:

- ❑ Length of the contract: whether you are hiring the trainer for a set number of days of work over a year or only for the duration of a programme.
- ❑ Role and responsibilities of the trainer.
- ❑ Fees: many companies pay a daily fee for course delivery, including travel to and from the venue (but not for preparation), as well as half the daily fee for participation in any train-the-trainers programmes. Fees could also be hourly, if relevant.
- ❑ Terms of payment.
- ❑ Terms of termination, in case the client cancels a programme or the trainer receives a poor evaluation from the client.
- ❑ Reimbursement of expenses (travel, accommodation, food, use of personal equipment such as computers or audiovisual).
- ❑ Expectations regarding preparation.
- ❑ Code of ethics.
- ❑ Copyright of training materials developed by the freelance trainer for the course.
- ❑ Confidentiality agreement regarding the client, the material and the participants.

Non-compete clauses are often included in the contract to ensure that the freelance trainer will not accept business from a client for whom he or she is working while under contract to you, for a given period of time. Indeed, freelance trainers often have their own company and business card, and will use the opportunity of being in a client's office to promote their own services. Frequently the client will ask the trainer to provide other services without going through you. Be clear with the freelance trainer about how you expect him or her to act in such a situation. You may, for instance, agree that he or she take on additional work from a client but pay you an introduction fee, since you did the hard work of obtaining that client in the first place. Or you can encourage their salesmanship by offering them a fee for any business that they bring to you, and hire them to deliver the training.

A good way to entice freelancers to actively participate in a network is to organize train-the-trainer sessions for them. The freelance consultant will realize the value of the relationship and will invest in it in return.

In many cases, the trainer may enhance the programme with personal material or tools. Be fair and acknowledge this input.

In some case, the client requests that the training company sign a confidentiality agreement because it may be privy to information, data, or technology that is sensitive and confidential. If you are operating in a legalistic society, you need to find out whether the freelance or staff trainer should sign the agreement too.

Evaluation

From the trainer's point of view, the purpose of evaluation is to get feedback from the participants on what worked, what didn't, and what needs to be improved. From the client's perspective (if the client is a company) the purpose of the evaluations is to assess what value was added to the company by an investment in training and to check the quality of the training service.

Too often, evaluations are little more than 'feel-good' exercises for both trainers and clients, and the data is never really analysed. For the data to be useful, the purpose of the evaluation must have been clearly defined. Trainees need to be made aware of its importance and fill it out conscientiously.

Evaluations can be done at different times either during or after the end of the course:

❏ On the spot, verbally;

❏ On the spot, in writing;

❏ A few days after the programme, when participants are back in the office;

❏ A few months after the programme, once the routine of work has resumed.

You can evaluate different things:

❏ The participants' knowledge and skills;

❏ The course;

❏ The training process.

Donald Kirkpatrick[6] has identified four levels of evaluation in order of complexity and importance:

❏ Level 1: Reaction;

❏ Level 2: Learning;

❏ Level 3: Behaviour;

❏ Level 4: Results.

Level 1 evaluation aims to elicit from the participants or client spontaneous reactions on the course, the process, the delivery and the training material.

Level 2 evaluation assesses what participants have learned from the course. Those two evaluation levels are carried out at the end of the course or within the next few days.

Level 3 evaluation targets behaviour change, asking whether participants are doing things differently on the job as a result of the training. Are these changes

---

6   Donald Kirkpatrick, *Evaluating Training Programmes*. Washington DC, American Society for Training and Development, 1975.

visible, can they be measured? To assess behaviour change, the feedback must often be given by third parties, that is, peers or supervisors. You can evaluate the demonstration of hard skills, soft skills, teamwork and so on.

Level 4 evaluation measures the results of behaviour change and how they affect the organization's effectiveness. This is often difficult to evaluate, because it is not obvious which improvements are attributable to training and which to other factors. Level 3 and level 4 evaluations are carried out several months after the end of the course. In many companies the human resources department will be responsible for both sending people on training and evaluating the effectiveness of training. They may delegate this responsibility to the trainer or training company if they have a close, long-term working relationship.

'On-the-spot' evaluations

At the end of the course, you should set aside a short period to receive feedback 'on the spot', either orally or in writing.

Oral evaluations are more interactive and you can ask for more clarifications or details than in written evaluation. Be aware that in some cultures participants will be reluctant to voice criticism, and you will therefore hear nothing but more or less sincere praise. Nonetheless, oral evaluations can be a pleasant way to bring closure to the programme.

Keep in mind that on-the-spot evaluations have certain limitations:

❑ They address the relevance and quality of the course but not the relevance of the training to the participant in his or her workplace;

❑ They are subjective;

❑ Participants have no critical distance from the course.

Written evaluations can be simple questionnaires (half a page) or more complex ones (but not longer than two pages). Several formats can be utilized; see the examples in appendix V. The questionnaires should aim to gather information about: pre-course communication, course setting, delivery, materials, and anything else that will be useful for you in designing future courses.

Questionnaire content

The questions should be simply worded, with one thought per question. Avoid complex questions like 'How good were the course materials (handouts, overheads, video, presentations, case studies ...)?' Instead formulate one question for each of the aspects you want feedback on.

The questions should go from specific to general. Do not start off with: 'How would you evaluate the overall quality of this programme?' It is better to build the big picture by starting with the components of what makes a good programme.

Questionnaires typically include questions about the following aspects of the course:

❑ Pre-course information: before the course did you receive sufficient information regarding the training objectives and the content?

❑ Material conditions of the course:
  – Quality of the venue.
  – Quality of the organization and logistics.

❑ Quality of the delivery and facilitation.

❏ Pace: did the course move too fast or too slow?

❏ Length: was the time allotted sufficient to address the content?

❏ Timing: was the course programmed too late, too early?

❏ Adequacy of target:

— Did this training answer your needs? (This question focuses on the trainees.)

— Have the objectives, as they were determined in the beginning of the training, been attained? (This formulation focuses on the delivery.)

❏ Overall satisfaction:

— Are you satisfied with the course?

— Would you recommend this course to somebody else?

Choosing the evaluation format

There are two types of information you can gather: qualitative and quantitative. Qualitative input will often be richer and include comments and suggestions, but will take longer to complete. Quantitative evaluations ask participants to rank aspects of the course on a scale. The answers can then be analysed and compared like an opinion poll. These ranking questions are also quick to fill out. You may choose to combine ranking questions with open-ended qualitative questions by asking trainees to justify their rankings.

Scales

There are several options for grading, depending on the number of grades you want in your scale; from 1 to 5 or from 1 to 4 generally gives you enough detail. You should prefer a grading scale that is familiar to the participants from school – these vary considerably from country to country. A few different options are proposed in table 11.

Table 11	5-step grading scales			
Very bad	**Bad**	**Average**	**Good**	**Very good**
– –	–	0	+	+ +
1(–)	2	3	4	5 (+)
E	D	C	B	A

❏ Even if it seems obvious to you, always qualify the number you use; in some cultures 1 is a good mark and 5 a poor mark, while elsewhere the opposite is true. If you use a numeric scale add a '–' or '+' sign to indicate the order.

❏ A scale of 1 to 4 does not offer a neutral answer (neither good nor bad) whereas in a scale of 5, the number 3 is often considered the neutral answer.

Another frequent question is whether the questionnaire should be anonymous or not. You may leave the decision to the participant by indicating that the form may be handed in anonymously, in which case they should not fill out the name field.

Accreditation

Delivering diplomas and certificates

Accreditation is a proof that the recipient has attained a certain level of skills and knowledge in a given area. High schools, universities, professional associations and many government bodies deliver accreditations to individuals, companies or institutions. Doctors, architects and teachers are all accredited, which give us the confidence to use their services in the knowledge that they will diagnose our illness correctly, build a solid house or teach our children well.

A diploma is an official document delivered by an institution accredited by the government, ministry of education or professional association to do so. The criteria for obtaining the diploma are set by a panel of experts. In order to be allowed to deliver diplomas, a training centre has to be reviewed and accredited by the relevant official institution.

However, in many countries there is little regulation or oversight of the training industry. Certificates and diplomas delivered by training centres may be worth little more than the paper they are written on. If this is the case, rather than delivering a diploma, which may give the trainee a misleading sense of the value of the certification, it is probably best to deliver a 'certificate of attendance'. This document is proof that the trainee has attended the course and completed it satisfactorily. The document should include the name of the trainee, the place, dates and title of the training course he or she attended, and be signed by the director of the training institution. These certificates also serve as a symbolic reward for completing the course.

Receiving accreditation as a training centre

As a trainer, you may use tools and tests that are the intellectual property of well-known institutions, which developed them and sell them. Often these institutions require you to be accredited to use their tools: this is the case for Positional Leadership training, Meyers Briggs, Herman Brain Dominance, and many others. To become accredited you need to follow a training course and show that you are fully capable of carrying out the process or analysis required to use the tool or test. You are then 'licensed' to use them and have access to computer data, updates or research as relevant. You may wish to investigate which tools you could profit from using and try to become accredited.

It is important, as a trainer and consultant, to respect the intellectual property of the processes or tools. Accreditation is a means of ensuring quality and avoiding misuse. Consultants and trainers earn a living from their intellect, and should be all the more respectful of intellectual property of others.

Appendix I

Areas of consulting

General management	Broad level or owner level management	❏ Setting or clarification of company objectives ❏ Company secretarial services ❏ Composition and procedures of board ❏ Corporate/strategic planning ❏ Management by objectives ❏ Planned management succession ❏ Growth planning ❏ Acquisition search and evaluation ❏ Divestment planning ❏ Policy formulation
	Executive level management	❏ Cost reduction programmes ❏ Economic studies ❏ Plant/branch location studies ❏ Management audit/SWOT analysis ❏ Management control systems ❏ Management development ❏ Systems planning and implementation ❏ Organizational structure ❏ Planning and control of projects ❏ Management development
Administrative management	Formation and registration of companies	
	Office administration	❏ Administration systems, development and control ❏ Organization and method studies
Financial management	Financial accounting	❏ Book keeping system ❏ Financial accounting system design ❏ Electronic accounting, computerization ❏ Cash-flow/working capital management ❏ Financial reporting

	Management accounting	❑ Cost accounting system ❑ Cost control ❑ Cost–volume price analysis ❑ Budgeting and budget control ❑ Financial analyses ❑ Long range planning ❑ Capital investment management
Plant engineering	Equipment/facility development	❑ Plan/layout engineering ❑ New equipment evaluation ❑ Plant rehabilitation/refurbishing ❑ Safety engineering
	Preventive maintenance planning	
Production management	Production methods	❑ Choice of technology or production process ❑ Production methods/process improvement ❑ Design of production aids/tools ❑ Good manufacturing practice ❑ Job redesign ❑ Work study, measurement and control ❑ Working conditions and improvement ❑ Incentives/productivity bonus schemes
	Production/process management	❑ Production planning and control ❑ Inventory planning and control ❑ Productivity improvement ❑ Quality control/assurance ❑ Waste control/utilization/management ❑ Environment control
	Techniques	❑ Operations research ❑ Total quality management ❑ Just in time ❑ Make/buy decisions ❑ Value analysis/engineering ❑ Network analysis ❑ System approach/development ❑ Standardization
Research and development	Product	❑ Product design/development ❑ Packaging development ❑ Raw material/component substitutes development ❑ Product life tests
	Process	❑ Process design/development/improvement ❑ Process control research
	R & D programme development	

Sales and marketing management	Sales management	❏ Sales planning and control ❏ Distribution management ❏ Sales force management ❏ Sales training
	Marketing management	❏ Market research ❏ Marketing audit ❏ Marketing organization ❏ New product development ❏ Product evaluation ❏ Marketing policy, planning and strategy development ❏ Marketing intelligence/consumer attitude research ❏ Sales analysis/forecasting ❏ Sales organization, planning and control ❏ Public relations management ❏ Marketing training
Technical services	Architectural design	
	Engineering design and installation	
	Technical studies and investigations	
	Appropriate technology	
	Technology transfer and upgrading	
Human resource management	Human resource development	❏ Executive search/selection and development ❏ Management training/staff training ❏ HRD planning ❏ Performance appraisal system development ❏ Executive counselling
	Personnel administration	❏ Payroll systems ❏ Salary review and administration ❏ Job design/evaluation ❏ Personnel policy formulation/planning/development ❏ Collective bargaining/industrial relations ❏ Vocational training ❏ Staff communication system

Computerization	System development	<ul><li>Feasibility studies</li><li>Hardware selection/planning</li><li>Software selection/development</li><li>Acquisition of computer services</li><li>Installation survey and appraisal</li><li>Programming</li><li>System analysis and design</li></ul>
	Computer training	
	Computer techniques	<ul><li>Computer aided design development</li><li>Computer aided manufacturing development</li><li>Management information systems</li><li>Flexible manufacturing systems</li><li>Optimized production technology</li><li>Just in time</li><li>Programme evaluation and review techniques</li><li>Operation research techniques</li><li>Simulated model testing</li></ul>
Management research and development	Investigations	<ul><li>Business valuation</li><li>Feasibility studies</li><li>Productivity measurements</li></ul>
	Research and development	<ul><li>Management practice and techniques</li><li>Socio-economic factors</li></ul>
Management external relations	Public relations	
	Third party affairs	
	Corporate interfacing	

Source: *Consultancy Handbook.* UNDP-ILO project RAS/86/070 prepared by Arvind Nande. Bangkok, October 1992.

Appendix II

Essential skills of consultants

Ethics and integrity	❑ Honesty
	❑ Confidentiality
	❑ Ability to place client's interest before one's own interest
	❑ Ability to recognize one's own limitations
	❑ Ability to admit mistakes and learn from them
	❑ Desire to help others
Intellectual ability	❑ Ability to learn quickly and easily
	❑ Ability to observe, gather, select and evaluate facts
	❑ Curiosity, reading and educating oneself
	❑ Good judgement
	❑ Instructive and deductive reasoning
	❑ Ability to synthesize and generalize
	❑ Creative imagination, original thinking
Objectivity	❑ Analytical mind
	❑ Good diagnostic ability
	❑ Ability to draw unbiased conclusions
	❑ Flexibility and adaptability to changed conditions
Interpersonal skills	❑ Respect for other people
	❑ Tolerance of others
	❑ Ability to adjust to different levels in the organization, from operators to top management
	❑ Ability to anticipate human reactions and evaluate them
	❑ Ability to gain trust and confidence of other people
	❑ Courtesy and good manners
Communication skills	❑ Listen
	❑ Convince
	❑ Facility in oral and written communication
	❑ Persuasion
	❑ Ability to motivate people
	❑ Ability to teach and train
Personal drive	❑ Initiative and self-reliance
	❑ Right degree of self confidence
	❑ Healthy ambition
	❑ Entrepreneurial spirit
	❑ Courage
	❑ Perseverance in action

Emotional maturity	❑ Stability of behaviour and action
	❑ Ability to withstand pressure and live with frustrations and uncertainties
	❑ Ability to act with poise and calm
	❑ Self-control in all situations
	❑ Flexibility and adaptability to changed situation

Source: *Consultancy Handbook.* UNDP-ILO project RAS/86/070 prepared by Arvind Nande. Bangkok, October 1992.

Training preparation checklist

Course name: _____

Date: _____ Location: _____

Before the course

Send confirmation letter to the company or the participants

Reserve the venue

- Main room
- Break-up rooms
- Number of participants
- Lodging
- Meals
- Coffee break
- Welcome drink
- Rules for drinks, mobile phones, etc. (for participants and for trainers)
- Inventory of equipment and materials needed, and who will provide
- Map of the venue, if large

Mail invitation letters

- To the participants only
  - Pre-course questionnaires
- To the trainers and participants
  - Location
  - How to get there (map, instructions)
  - Date, time
  - List of participants
  - All documentation
  - Payment conditions

Prepare the room

- Keys and closing information
- Room set-up
- Welcome desk
- Handouts
- Evaluation forms
- Flip charts

- Name tags or name cards
- Water, glasses
- Office equipment (sellotape, scissors, etc.)
- Writing pads, pens
- Lots of extra markers, chalk

Media and audiovisual

- Overhead projector
- Video
- Camera
- Video projector
- Cassettes
- Microphones
- Extension cords
- Adapters
- Computer
    - Portable
    - Printer

After the course

- Evaluation form
- Update list of participants
- Follow up with participants
- Send invoice to client

Appendix IV

Pre-course questionnaires

Pre-course questionnaire 1

Course title: [*insert name of course*]

Name: _____

Organization: _____ Position: _____

Purpose of the course:

[*To be completed by the trainer: explain who the course is addressed to and what its objectives are.*]

Purpose of the questionnaire:

[*To be completed by the trainer: explain how the questionnaire is designed to help target the content of the course to the trainees needs.*]

Please complete this questionnaire and return it by [*insert date*] to: [*insert trainer's or training company's address*].

1. Who suggested you attend this course and/or how did you hear about it?
    _____
    _____

2. What do you do in your present position that justifies your attending, or what motivates your interest in this course?
    _____
    _____

3. Which areas of the course programme do you know most about?
    _____
    _____

4. Which areas of the course programme do you know least about?
    _____
    _____

5. What do you expect to take away from this course?
    _____
    _____

6. Do you have any further comments, requests or ideas for this course?
    _____
    _____

Thank you for taking the time to answer this questionnaire.

Pre-course questionnaire 2

Course title: *[insert name of course]*

Please complete this questionnaire to help us in our course planning, and forward the completed questionnaire by *[insert date]* to: *[insert trainer's or training company's address]*.

1. Please provide your personal details:

Last name: _____   First name: _____

Company: _____   Department: _____

Position: _____

Address: _____

Telephone: _____   Fax: _____   E-mail: _____

2.   List any course on *[insert course subject]* that you have taken. Include short courses, workshops, seminars, etc. Describe the target audience for these courses.

   Course title   Target audience

   _____
   _____
   _____
   _____

3.   What knowledge and skills would you like to acquire at this course?

   _____
   _____
   _____
   _____

4.   Can this knowledge or skills be applied in your workplace or other activities? If so, how?

   _____
   _____
   _____
   _____

Thank you for taking the time to answer this questionnaire.

Evaluation questionnaires

One-minute feedback

This evaluation is a quick 'temperature check'. You can use it at the end of each session of a course. It can be used when running a pilot of a new training programme.

Evaluation questionnaire

Session or course name: _____   Date: _____

On a scale of 1(+) to 5(−) please rank the following aspects of the course or session:

So far I'm finding this course to be (circle your answer)…

Interesting	1	2	3	4	5	Uninteresting
Too fast	1	2	3	4	5	Too slow
Too easy	1	2	3	4	5	Too difficult
Relevant	1	2	3	4	5	Irrelevant
Organized	1	2	3	4	5	Disorganized
Relaxed	1	2	3	4	5	Tense

Please tell us how you think the course could be improved:

_____

_____

_____

_____

_____

Your name (optional): _____

Thank you for taking the time to answer this questionnaire.

Session highs and lows

This type of quick evaluation can be use to get feedback at the end of each course or training-programme session (e.g. half day, day).

Evaluation questionnaire

Course title: _____   Date: _____

Session topic: _____

Please give use your feedback about today's course session. The more specific your answers, the more helpful they will be to us in improving the course.

What did you find most interesting about the course/session?

_____

_____

_____

_____

_____

What did you find least interesting about the course/session?

_____

_____

_____

_____

Do you have any suggestions for improving this course?

_____

_____

_____

_____

Your name (optional): _____

Thank you for taking the time to answer this questionnaire.

Reflections and application planning

This informal approach mixes reflections about learning with thinking about how the knowledge and skills will be applied. It is useful when training is done on the job or in work-like situations.

Evaluation questionnaire

Course title: _____   Date: _____

1.   What are two skills that you have gained or strengthened at this course?

(a) _____

_____

_____

(b) _____

_____

_____

2.   What one thing are you going to do differently next week, or sooner, as a result of something you learned on the course?

_____

_____

_____

_____

_____

3.   Name one or two people whom you will encourage to learn what you've learned in this course.

_____

_____

_____

_____

_____

Your name (optional): _____

Thank you for taking the time to answer this questionnaire.

Mixed evaluation

The following two questionnaires are examples of mixed evaluation: they ask the trainee to rank certain aspects of the course, but also to provide qualitative input.

This is a sample questionnaire from a training programme aimed at developing negotiating skills for export managers. Quantitative evaluation allows you to compare reactions among participants across different workshops. Asking why after each question helps clarify the rating.

Evaluation questionnaire

Course name: Developing Negotiating Skills for Export Managers

Date: _____

Rate the following aspects of the course on a scale 1 to 5 (1 = Low, 5 = High) and briefly outline the reasons for your rating.

1.   How would you rate this course in terms of its value to you individually?

                   (–)1   2   3   4   5(+)

    Why?

    _____

    _____

2.   How would you rate this course in term of its value for your organization?

                  1   2   3   4   5

    Why?

    _____

    _____

3.   Did the course provide sufficient negotiation practice?

                  1   2   3   4   5

    What was most useful?

    _____

    What was least useful?

    _____

    _____

4.   How useful was feedback during the practice session?

                  1   2   3   4   5

    Why?

    _____

    _____

5.   Has your confidence as a negotiator improved?

                  1   2   3   4   5

    Why?

    _____

    _____

6.   I received valuable insights, modes and suggestions for:

- Preparing my negotiation.
  (disagree strongly)   1   2   3   4   5 (agree strongly)

- Understanding my counterpart's culture.
  (disagree strongly)   1   2   3   4   5 (agree strongly)

- Adjusting my negotiation style.
  (disagree strongly)   1   2   3   4   5 (agree strongly)

- Being creative in unblocking the negotiation.
  (disagree strongly)   1   2   3   4   5 (agree strongly)

Do you have any other comments?

_____

_____

_____

Thank you for taking the time to answer this questionnaire.

Mixed evaluation: second example

This form is adapted from a questionnaire developed and used by Shell Canada Limited, Calgary, Alberta, Canada.

Training programme evaluation

Name: _____   Date: _____

Course title: _____

Course leader(s) name: _____

Please circle the appropriate response.

Stated outcomes were achieved during the training programme:

      Not at all   Somewhat   Completely
      1   2   3   4   5   6   7   8   9

Training programme content was relevant and challenging.

      Not at all   Somewhat   Completely
      1   2   3   4   5   6   7   8   9

Support materials (e.g. handouts) were helpful.

      Not at all   Somewhat   Completely
      1   2   3   4   5   6   7   8   9

The training programme leader was effective.

      Not at all   Somewhat   Completely
      1   2   3   4   5   6   7   8   9

This training programme has improved my understanding of the topic.

      Not at all   Somewhat   Very much
      1   2   3   4   5   6   7   8   9

This training programme has equipped me with information and skills that I can use immediately.

      Not at all   Somewhat   Very much
      1   2   3   4   5   6   7   8   9

The time allowed for the training programme was …

      Too little   Sufficient   Too much

Overall the course was:

      Very poor   Fine   Excellent
      1   2   3   4   5   6   7   8   9

Highlights – What parts of the training programme were most interesting and useful for you?

_____

_____

_____

Low points – What parts of the training programme were of little or no value for you?

_____

_____

_____

Leadership – Comment on the training programme leader's effectiveness (e.g. rapport with group, presentation, methods and models used).

_____

_____

_____

Other comments – Do you have any other comments and suggestions that were not addressed by this questionnaire?

_____

_____

_____

Thank you for taking the time to answer this questionnaire.

Mixed evaluation: third example

Evaluation questionnaire

Date: _____

Name: _____

Course leader(s) name: _____

1. How would you assess the quality of the information you received about this programme?

    Very bad   1   2   3   4   5   Very good

2. Was the information you received about the training programme consistent with what was actually delivered?

    Not at all   1   2   3   4   5   Completely

3. Was the content of the training programme relevant and challenging?

    Not at all   1   2   3   4   5   Completely

4. Were support material and handouts helpful?

    Not at all   1   2   3   4   5   Completely

5. How effective were the programme leaders?

    [*Name of leader*]   Very poor   1   2   3   4   5   Very good

    [*Name of leader*]   Very poor   1   2   3   4   5   Very good

6. Has the training programme equipped you with information and skills that you can use immediately?

    Not at all   1   2   3   4   5   Completely

7. The programme had [*insert number*] workshops of [*insert duration*] days each. How was the time allocated for each course?

    Too little   About right   Too much

8. How would you assess the overall quality of this programme?

    Very poor   1   2   3   4   5   Excellent

9. What parts of the course were most interesting to you?

    _____

    _____

    _____

10. What parts of the training had little or no value to you?

_____

_____

_____

11. What would you recommend we change in the overall delivery (sequence of each course)?

_____

_____

_____

12. Comment on the effectiveness of the delivery (rapport with the group, presentation, methods and models used). What do we need to improve?

_____

_____

_____

13. Other comments

_____

_____

_____

Thank you for taking the time to answer this questionnaire.

Thematic bibliography

On adult learners

Argyris, Chris. *On Organizational Learning.* Cambridge, Blackwell, 1993.

_____ *Overcoming Organization Defenses: Facilitating organizational learning.* Boston, Allyn and Bacon, 1990.

_____ 'Teaching smart people how to learn.' *Harvard Business Review*, May-June 1991.

Brown, Rupert. *Group Processes: Dynamics within and between groups.* Oxford, Blackwell, 1988.

Knowles, Malcolm. *The Adult Learner: A neglected species.* 3rd ed. Houston, Gulf Publishing, 1984.

Kolb, David A. *Experiential Learning: Experience as the source for learning and development.* Englewood Cliffs, N.J., Prentice Hall, 1984.

Lewin, Kurt. *A Dynamic Theory of Personality.* New York, McGraw-Hill, 1959.

Mucchielli, Roger. *La dynamique des groupes.* Paris, ESF Éditeur, 1994.

Napier, Rodney and Matti K. Gershenfeld. *Making Groups Work: A guide for group leaders.* Boston, Houghton Mifflin, 1983.

Senge, Peter M. *The Fifth Discipline: The art and practice of the learning organization.* New York, Doubleday, 1990.

Senge, Peter M. *and others. The Fifth Discipline Fieldbook: Strategies and tools for building a learning organization.* London, Nicholas Bealey, 1994.

Smith, Donna M. and David A. Kolb. *The User's Guide for the Learning Styles Inventory: A manual for teacher and trainer.* Boston, McBeer and Co., 1986.

Zemke, Ron and Susan Zemke. '30 things we know for sure about adult learning'. *Training*, June 1981.

On consulting

Bens, Ingrid. *Facilitation at a Glance.* Salem NH, GOAL/QPC and the Association for Quality and Participation (AQP), 1999.

Brassard, Michael and Diane Ritter. *The Memory Jogger^{TM}: A pocket guide of tools for continuous improvement and effective planning.* Salem, NH, GOAL/QPC, 1999.

Consultancy Handbook. UNDP-ILO Project RAS 86/070, Bangkok, October 1992.

Damelio, Robert. *The Basics of Process Mapping.* Portland, Productivity Inc., 1996.

Greiner, Larry and Danielle Nees. 'Conseils en management : tous les mêmes?' *Revue française de gestion*, No. 75, November-December 1989.

Kubr, Milan. *Management Consulting: A guide to the profession.* 4th ed. Geneva, International Labour Organization, 1998.

Schein, Edgar, H. *Process Consulting: Its roles in organizational development.* Reading, MA, Addison-Wesley, 1969.

On training in general

Barzucchetti, S. et J.-F. Claude. *Évaluation de la formation et performance de l'entreprise.* Paris, Éditions Liaisons, 1995.

Bazin, Roger. *Organiser les sessions de formation.* Paris, ESF Éditeur, 1996.

Beau, Dominique. *La boîte à outils du formateur.* Paris, Éditions d'organizations, 2000.

Bacon, Stephen. *The Conscious use of Metaphor in Outward Bound.* Denver, Colorado Outward Bound School, 1983.

Clark, Ruth C. *Developing Technical Training: A structured approach for the development of classroom and computer-based instructional materials.* Reading, MA, Addison-Wesley, 1989.

Guidelines for Writing Business Cases: Studies in developing countries. Geneva, International Trade Centre, 1998.

Guide pratique de la formation. Paris, ESF Éditeur, 2001.

Martin, Jean-Paul and Emile Savary. *Intervenir en formation.* Lyon, Chronique sociale, 1998.

Mayo, G. Douglas and Philip H. Dubois. *The Complete Book of Training: Theory, Principles and Techniques.* San Diego, University Associates, 1987.

Messinger, Joseph. *Ces gestes qui vous trahissent.* Paris, First Editions, 1999.

Miller ,Vincent A. *The Guidebook for International Trainers in Business and Industry.* New York, Van Nostrand Reinhold, 1979.

Munson, Lawrence. *How to Conduct Training Seminars.* New York, McGraw-Hill, 1984.

Odiorne, George S. and Geary A. Rummler. *Training and Development: A guide for professionals.* Chicago, Commerce Clearing House Inc., 1988.

Pepper, Allan. *Managing the Training and Development Function.* London, Gower, 1985.

Pike, Robert W. *Creative Training Techniques Handbook.* Minneapolis, Lakewood Books, 1989.

Repplier, Ann D. 'A study of verbal influence strategies for reducing group resistance in consultation and training.' Unpublished PHD thesis. Temple University, 1986.